The
Codex

The Codex

A Divine Writ

VOLUME I

Cyrus Rumi

Matador
9 De Montfort Mews
Leicester LE1 7FW, UK
Tel: (+44) 116 255 9311 / 9312
Email: books@troubador.co.uk
Web: www.troubador.co.uk/matador

ISBN 978-1906221-195

Typeset in 12pt Bembo by Troubador Publishing Ltd, Leicester, UK
Printed in the UK by The Cromwell Press Ltd, Trowbridge, Wilts, UK

Matador is an imprint of Troubador Publishing Ltd

The Codex is dedicated to those seeking inner
truths, spiritual wisdom, human compassion
and love.

Preface

This is a book, which I have decided to name *The Codex,* and which contains a series of revelations intended for those who are spiritually inclined and wishing to experience the world from a slightly different theological perspective. It speaks to individuals, communities and nations on many levels; individually and collectively, spiritually and rationally. Importantly, you need not be necessarily disposed to any particular belief system or religious tradition to benefit from the readings contained in this book. *The Codex* is all embracing and welcomes readers who profess no faith at all. Enjoy the readings from both subjective and objective perspectives. Appreciate the subtle nuances that come to your awareness, serving to strengthen your spiritual experiences and journey into the mysteries of the unknown.

It has been my humble intention not to offend anyone intentionally. Some communications (revelations) have been deliberately left out so as to not to offend the sensibilities of some readers as they were considered too inflammatory to be included in *The Codex* at this moment in time. Perhaps one day I shall include them in my later volumes, when the state of world affairs becomes more stable, less volatile and more humane than it is at the present time.

The Codex is intended to be read and discussed widely and it is sincerely hoped it will be of use to a large cross-section of humanity of diverse persuasions. A universally accepted text that makes no distinction between *believers* and *non-believers*, it may contradict some of the views you have held or currently hold. But my personal recommendation is to see through these superficialities and explore the greater picture that these revelations present to humanity and to you, the kind reader. It must be stressed that this is no normal book as I will very briefly attempt to explain below.

In fact, when I first contemplated writing this preface I was uncertain as to how to structure it and what was required of me to introduce the reader to this fascinating area of spiritual awareness, personal growth and revelations. I was tempted not to write anything, but allow *The Codex* to explain itself. But then I realized that to write something like this would require some thoughtful explanations so that the reader could fully appreciate the teachings it contained and not be put off by the apparent disjointed style of presentation and content.

What follows is a fictional question and answer format to elucidate my humble intentions. I hope you will find it useful and full of insight. With time, I intend to expand further this preface from the expected feedback I hope to receive from the readers. But for now, I hope you will find the following elucidation useful.

How did this book come about?
This whole process I found personally very strange. It all started when I was travelling to work very early in the morning. While travelling in my car, I would have a thought or feeling that would enter my consciousness. It would be totally out of the blue and unrelated to what I was doing or thinking at the time. It would be always of a spiritual or religious dimension. As time progressed these thoughts would intrude into my consciousness at any time of the day, e.g. watching T.V., in the gym, while working on my assignments, to mention only a few.

To cut a long story short, I noticed a particular pattern to these thoughts, and some years later began to write them down. This allowed me to more attentive to the thoughts and feelings, by writing them down and documenting them with dates. My only deep regret is that I failed to write these thoughts down when I first became conscious of them. And so, as a consequence, there may be over a thousand communications that have not been documented. Some of them, I know for a fact, were very profound and soul-searching. Perhaps they will come to me at a later date in my life.

But importantly, it was not the case of me hearing voices from a burning bush in the desert, or being visited by an angel with wings in some deep recesses of a mountain cave. Far from it, these experiences felt very normal, natural, and comforting. This probably partially explains why in my earlier days I ignored the importance of recording these communications in any form.

A further point that is worth mentioning is that the readings in *The Codex* are not the actual words that have surfaced from the depths of my consciousness. They only represent a general free paraphrased translation of my experiential thoughts and an attempt to translate that which is untranslatable. In fact, it is my strong opinion that no translation is ever adequate and this is primarily due to the limitations intrinsic in the written word. I hope this subtle clarification will dispel any misunderstandings that may arise in the reader's mind with regard to the accuracy of the revelations contained in *The Codex*.

Why were you and not someone else chosen to be the recipient of such revelations?
In fact, my take on this matter is very simple. I think everyone has this innate capacity to become a recipient of these types of communications. Perhaps, some are more attuned than others. It's just a matter of getting in touch with your inner self and recognising what surfaces from your subconscious. Perhaps, at this

stage in my personal and unique journey in life, I have a greater awareness than say, my gardener. That's not to say that he or she lacks the innate potential. But perhaps he's not ready for it yet. I really don't know the answer to this question. Perhaps, one day I shall know the truth of the matter with a greater clarity of mind.

Can we trust your message?
Well, the ultimate decision resides with yourselves. Let's put it this way. I'm no charlatan; nor am I intentionally trying to deceive humanity. You'll just have to take my word for it. You could argue that I may be mentally deranged or suffering from some other ailment of the mind, like psychosis. That is your prerogative. But if that is the case, then please do inform my general practitioner. He may wish to run some tests before having me sectioned under the Mental Health Act should he think I'm a danger to others and myself!

But on a serious note. The same can be said about other great and not so great figures in history. The choice is really yours and how comfortable you feel about things that may appear at first instance very alien to your particular belief system. I would say pick and choose what you like, provided you feel comfortable with it. And, perhaps, do not be so judgmental in your first reading of *The Codex*. Allow yourselves to think about what is being related, and perhaps not come to immediate or hasty conclusions. Read *The Codex* with an open mind.

How do we know that you are not possessed by some evil or demonic force to create confusion in the minds of the believers?
I am in no authoritative position to answer this question to the satisfaction of those intent in finding fault with these readings and myself. I can only say that you should read the material with an open mind and follow the whispers of your conscience. If you disagree with anything, just ignore it, and go

onto the next reading. There is no compulsion to follow the guidance contained in *The Codex*. This is because the path one takes to self-awareness is unique to you.

However, I do sincerely hope you find *The Codex* useful and enlightening in many aspects of your own personal lives. As I said earlier, pick and choose that which is agreeable to yourselves and your belief systems. The primary message that appears to echo in *The Codex* is to believe in yourselves and that everything else will come secondary to this belief. A fundamental belief in a God, gods or goddesses is not a requirement to personal salvation.

Are you claiming to be a prophet or some saint or holy man?
The answer to this is an emphatic no. I am no different from any ordinary person in the street. I am a mortal, with strengths and weaknesses, like the rest of humanity. But I do think I have a special gift of experiencing things pertaining to spiritual matters that others may not be so at ease with, or lack a receptiveness that may be considered as a prerequisite to unlocking the doors of the heavenly kingdom of our imagination.

Nor do I wish to compare myself with great figures in history like Moses, Buddha, Jesus, Muhammad, Guru Nanak, Bahaullah or the many great saints within the ancient traditions of Hinduism, Paganism and other ancient belief systems. They all served an invaluable role in their communities.

What if some of the teachings do not agree with my religious traditions?
If you are not ready to accept some of the teachings then, as I said earlier, simply ignore them for the moment. But don't just rubbish them out of hand. Make a note of them, and then refer back to them at a later date, when you think you will be able

to give them a more serious, generous and objective rendering.

How did you come about choosing the name of this book?
I personally liked the word *The Codex* (which may be loosely translated as *The Manuscript*). It just entered into my consciousness when I was engaged in some mundane task. I hope it is a name that people can easily remember and utter when referring to this monumental work in the making.

How should we go about reading the text?
You don't have to read *The Codex* in any particular order. Simply open the book randomly and just read the particular reading or readings. If you wish to follow it from beginning to end then that is perfectly fine. *The Codex* is intended to be a very robust form of spiritual information for those interested in the realm of religion and spirituality, and should be read with this mindset.

Why does it feel a little disjointed? Why does it not read like a normal story book or biblical scriptures?
The very nature of revelations and communications dictates that it will not read like, say, a novel or a history book. They take place at anytime, under different circumstances and are not scripted like a play. The purpose of *The Codex* is to relay direct and indirect communications in a style that is closely authentic to the original message.

And don't forget that I'm no novelist, writer or journalist wishing to make a lot of money. This is not intended to be a literary masterpiece. I just wish to share with others what I believe belongs to them. I leave it to others to cast their judgment on *The Codex*.

Also note that sometimes a reading may be contextually based.

But it should not prevent you from reading it out of context and applying it to your own particular context and situation. This allows these revelations to take on a more universal dimension and appeal.

Why does some of the material seem very familiar in The Codex?
If it didn't feel familiar then I would feel a little worried and concerned. The fact is that much of the material is a continuum of much earlier teachings. The key thing to note is that the process of revelations is a continuous process that never ceases. If this was the case then it would raise more troubling philosophical questions than answers about the whole nature of revelations. I think I'll leave it at that for now, before it becomes too academic.

Why is this volume one?
This is because I haven't yet written volume two! In fact, at present, I do have enough material to write several volumes of equal size to the present volume. Initially, I wish to gauge the popularity of this present volume before embarking on publishing the other volumes.

What will be the content of volume two? And how many volumes of The Codex will there be in total?
The content will be very similar to the present volume. By that I mean it will appeal to the spiritual dimensions of human existence. It will, naturally, be varied and touch on various aspects of life in general.

The total number of volumes to be published is unknown to myself. This is because, as I said above, that the actual process of communications or a revelation is a continuous process. Not bound by time or space. And I don't imagine these will cease until I draw my very last breath. In the future, the job of collating these communications will be left to those who wish to publish and disseminate them for the general public consumption. And this is based on the assumption that there will be a sincere desire and hunger for such spiritual guidance, as contained in *The Codex*.

In one of the future volumes I have the humble intention of including the communications that I found very ambiguous, troubling and which related to future events. I thought there was no advantageous purpose in including them so early on in this present volume. However, a few have inadvertently appeared in this present volume, which I have decided to retain.

What are your personal intentions and aims for The Codex?
I hope some publishing company takes the gamble and decides to publish the material on a grand scale. Distributed throughout the world and translated into various languages. Bound in various formats, e.g., small pocket versions; children's versions with graphic pictures that complement the readings. And, perhaps, a small percentage of the sales to be donated to a reputable charity that primarily promotes the genuine welfare of people and encourages education.

But perhaps I'm being a little too unrealistic and naive. Then surely, there is nothing wrong in dreaming of what can be achieved, provided it's not too unrealistic! You never know, it could end up in a museum in hundred or so years from now! But the thing to remember is that *The Codex* is not only about me but about us, you, yourselves and the journey we decide to take in life – individually and collectively. I genuinely believe *The Codex* provides the blueprint to the life you may wish to live or at least consider.

I personally believe there is great potential for *The Codex* to do great good in a world that appears chaotic and lacks direction and spirituality. I can only leave it in the hands of others to see where and to what level they can take this book and its humble message.

I now take leave and ask the kind reader to engage with an open mind the readings that follow. Allow the teachings to guide you on a journey of personal spiritual development. It is a journey, I sincerely believe, you will not regret.

Revelations I

Revelation 1

Let this communication be recorded and shared
with those who entertain an open mind.
Let this communication be shared
with those overflowing with love and compassion
within themselves.
Let this communication serve as a guide
for those of understanding and reason.
So be it!

Revelation 2

Through Me,
you shall attain divinity!
Through Me,
you shall see, evolve and emerge
through the veils of light and darkness.
Through Me,
you shall become one with the eternal.
Be not troubled or fearful.
Be steadfast.
This is My promise to you all.

Revelation 3

I speak to you all,
but it is up to you to recognise and experience
My presence, thoughts and feelings.

I exist independently of the perceived constraints of
time and space.
I am present in dimensions
outside your human comprehension.
But each one of you
can experience Me.
And I you.

Be not afraid!
Allow yourselves to gravitate
and merge into Me.
And I shall gravitate
and merge into you.

Meet Me halfway,
and I shall fully embrace you
in My divine love.
Just leave the rest to Me,
and be not fearful
of the truth.

And I say again:
Be not afraid!
Allow your inner serenity to
expand and blossom within you.
Allow the serenity that exists in the outer realm
to descend upon and enter your being.

I never break My promises.
So place your trust in Me.

Revelation 4

All will be well,
if you perceive it to be so!
All will be well,
if you perceive it to be so!
All will be well,
if you perceive it to be so!
I have spoken.

Revelation 5

Many have seen Me,
but only a few have experienced Me.

Revelation 6

My divine presence is like the ocean
where the creatures of the sea
are oblivious to the boundaries of their realm.

Revelation 7

Oh humanity!
Wherever you may be,
you cannot escape your own physical immortality.
No place on earth remains untouched
by the ravages of time, decay and death.
Recognise the nature of such impermanence,
so that you may realise your true and unique relationship
with your surroundings.
Knowing this
shall lead you to the path that leads to
greater understanding, true love and compassion.

Revelation 8

The essence of truth;
the essence of reality;
the essence of life;
the essence of immortality.
They are all present within you.
You just need time, patience and deep reflection
to recognise them.

Revelation 9

Oh humanity!
Know that you all are connected on many levels.
So do not be of those
who discriminate against one another.
For those who do are,
in fact, discriminating against themselves,
and Me.
If you wish to be true to yourselves,
and Me,
then be friends to all things
so that which is divine within yourselves
may grow and blossom.

Revelation 10

See Me in all things.
Experience and perceive Me in all things.
Hear Me in all things.

Revelation 11

You cannot comprehend My vastness
through intellect alone.
It is through deep reflective meditation
and inner experience
that you can attain personal truths about Me.

Revelation 12

Oh humanity!
Each of you worships a different personal God
dependent upon your unique individual understanding.
The perceived God of one person
is not the same as the perceived God of another.
This is because you all attribute a unique and different quality
to My eternal persona.
This is acceptable
and you should not make distinctions in such matters.
As it will only lead you to
bigotry, wars and mental confusion.
Chaos will reign
and prevail over all that is good.

I have many attributes,
so choose what you may in your journey
to understanding Me and yourselves.
Discriminate against no one,
or by your very deeds,
you will become the victim of your own discrimination.
It is your actions
that will determine your spiritual fate.

Revelation 13

You shall not attain any spiritual worth
if you are unable to cultivate
and share compassion with others,
including animals.
Respect all sentient life forms.
Address these issues
before you knock on the doors
of My kingdom.

Revelation 14

Be just in your dealings with others.
Display honesty in your actions.
Be compassionate, loving and benevolent to all sentient forms.
In so doing,
your actions will echo in all of eternity,
acting as a shield against your perceived fears.
And I shall be with you all the time.
Till the end of time,
and beyond.

Revelation 15

Oh people of understanding!
Where there is complexity,
seek out simplicity.
Where there is diversity,
seek out unity.
Where there is chaos and disorder,
seek out order and harmony.
And all else is superfluous.

Revelation 16

Those of you who have been touched by true love
have nothing to fear in this world,
nor in the hereafter.
They are the blessed ones.

Revelation 17

The blessed shall be the inheritors of all that is esoteric,
and more.
This is My promise to you.

Revelation 18

Look beyond the realm of words and rituals
so that you may save yourselves
from ignorance and anarchy.

Revelation 19

Swim in My ocean of love
and submerge yourself in the mystery
that is life itself.
Experience the pure serenity
of mind, soul and body
that arises from deep within.

Revelation 20

Allow that which is Me
to become that which is you.
Allow My experiences
to become your experiences.
Let us become one in this celestial union
so that you are able to see through My eyes
and I through yours.
And let this holy marriage be celebrated
by those of wisdom
and esoteric knowledge.

Revelation 21

In meditating on My eternal essence,
permit your mind to empty all that which presents within.
Discard the debris by the wayside
and enter My domain
with the innocence and simplicity of a newborn infant.
Only then will you experience
that which is divine from within.
Only then will you appreciate with greater awareness
My dormant state within your deepest being.
Recognising its resourcefulness
and allowing it to grow, expand and blossom
so that eventually you and I become eternally one
and whole.

Revelation 22

You can never be truly independent
from the eternal oneness of My being.
You can never be independent
from the collective
that simply exists outside
the perceived dimensional parameters.
This is the eternal state of affairs.

Revelation 23

I am all that you experience.
I am who I am.
At peace and in equilibrium with all manifestations,
seen and unseen.
Present across all known
and unknown dimensions.

Revelation 24

When you begin to merge
from a lower reality into that which is higher,
you shall begin to lose attachment
to the material elements of your existence.
As this phase progresses
you will attain greater awareness
of the ever present realities of life itself.
And the doors of My kingdom
will be ever near.

Revelation 25

When you experience Me within yourselves,
you shall realise that belief systems
no longer hold the same sway
over your minds, souls and bodies.
Your mental bondage will cease to exist
as you become conscious of the eternal truth
of My presence within yourselves.
An open access to the truth.

Revelation 26

Be not of those who degrade their humanity
by following their base instincts.
Elevate yourselves above the station of animals
by showing love, compassion and rational conduct
in all your affairs.
In so doing,
you shall recognise My divine presence.
In so doing,
you will appreciate life itself.

Revelation 27

Ignorance is the fuel that bolsters your false egos
and your corrupt desires.

Revelation 28

Use your mind and body
for the good of all things.

Revelation 29

Oh humanity!
There is no need to be submerged
in perceived guilt and self-pity.
It will only serve to hinder and destroy
your spiritual growth from within.
Allow yourselves to be accepting of the circumstances.

Let the inner voice from within
guide you to a higher level of consciousness in Me.
And in so doing,
your perceived guilt will be vanquished.
Starting afresh,
like a newborn,
with a pure blank slate of innocence.

Revelation 30

Blessed are those of you who can
remain unattached to the fruits of your actions.
Expecting nothing from others,
yourself and Me.
This includes your perceptions and expectations from Me
about events that shall unfold in the hereafter.
With such a frame of mind,
you shall be blessed with serenity wherever you may be.
Destroying the ego
which once overwhelmed every part of your being.
Dissipating its negative force
until it no longer threatens your spiritual well-being.
And when your ego no longer threatens you,
you shall find great moments from within
where you are pleasantly surprised
with ecstatic joy, hope and love.
This is My promise to you.

Revelation 31

I work through you.
And you work through Me.
So be content in this life of yours
and that which is to follow.
Expect nothing from life itself.
In this way you shall never be disheartened,
nor shall you grieve.

Revelation 32

Oh humanity!
Appreciate the knowledge
that I and you are made of the same fundamental substance.
For those with intellect and wisdom,
ponder and reflect upon this.
Those with esoteric insight
shall know the truth of My communications.

Revelation 33

I am order,
and chaos is its antithesis.
Ponder and reflect upon this.

Revelation 34

The Apocalypse that some of you seek out,
and that others dread,
is but a projection of the turmoil
that persists within your inner realm.
First, act to comprehend that which is within.
And only then shall you have the doors opened to you
pertaining to that which you seek in your traditions.

Revelation 35

I am eternal
since I perceive Myself to be eternal.
And all else is mere conjecture.

Revelation 36

Oh humanity!
Why do some of you proclaim the right to take the lives
of the adulterers, adulteresses and the fornicators
so that you can appease My perceived wrath!

Oh ignorant ones!
What real purpose will taking a life serve?
Will you not, in the process of taking a life,
be also culpable of taking Mine too?
Can you not comprehend and experience the irrationality
of those who preach and propagate such doctrines?

Oh people!
Refrain from such acts
if you wish to embrace compassion and true love for all.
Refrain from such acts
if you wish to be overflowing with My Holy Spirit.
For surely,
those of you who are filled with My essence
cannot be guilty of such lowly beast-like acts!

Revelation 37

The less you possess
the more rich you are from within.
Ponder and reflect upon this.

Revelation 38

Know that
you shall all become barren dust
at the end of your earthly journey.
So what prevents you
from being loving and compassionate?
And what prevents you
from performing noble deeds
that may echo in the vastness of eternity?

Revelation 39

Oh humanity!
Your earthly sojourn is but a short span
compared to that which awaits you in My kingdom.
Spend the time you have
in doing good to others
and keeping out of trouble and mischief.
And if violence confronts you,
then walk away.
Wishing no ill on the perpetrators of hate and violence.
Time itself will deal with them
in the most appropriate manner.

Revelation 40

You reap whatever you have sown.
So do not victimise the innocent,
the poor and the needy.

Revelation 41

Oh humanity!
In the true nature of things,
you are neither born,
nor do you die.
You simply exist and experience.
Ponder and reflect upon this.

Revelation 42

Simply 'be',
and your lives will become meaningful.
Simply 'be',
and all mysteries shall cease to perplex.
Simply 'be',
and you shall experience perfection.
Simply 'be',
and you shall encompass eternity.
Simply 'be',
and you shall attain Godhood.
This is My promise to you.

Revelation 43

People of true inner faith, wisdom and knowledge
have no fear
of that which lurks in the unknown;
or the known.
They walk the earth
with serenity of mind and body.
They follow the middle path.

Revelation 44

Allow the eternal inner compassion
and love that resides within yourselves
to displace counterproductive fears,
anxieties and bigotry.
Let true understanding prevail
and flourish.
And in so doing,
the essence of life
will itself blossom.

Revelation 45

Life is that which predates time.
And life is the essence
which shall exist
when time folds on itself.
That which exists
in its purest and simplest form.
A unique mystery in itself.
And those of you who have attained esoteric understanding
have experienced the beauty of this majestic mystery.
Both I and you
are humbled by its essence.

Revelation 46

Oh humanity!
Do you know what binds you and Me?
It is the eternal essence
of life itself.
Be not surprised by such revelations.
The truth can sometimes be difficult
to comprehend and accept.
This is understandable to some
and incomprehensible to others.

Revelation 47

Enjoy life
without your self-imposed inhibitions.
Life is to be enjoyed to its fullest,
even at moments of
perceived pain and sorrow.
But bring no harm to others
in this process of enjoyment.
Enjoy!
Enjoy!
Enjoy!

Revelation 48

I am peace and happiness.
So bring peace and happiness
to all you encounter.

Oh people!
The truly rich amongst humanity
is one who does not make material wealth
their prime reason for living.
It is a false source of perceived happiness
and fulfilment.

Oh people!
Wealth is fleeting
and only serves to prop up
your false egos.
Those of wisdom and knowledge
remain indifferent to what good
or bad fortune befalls them.
They remain focussed
on elevating their own inner awareness
so that they may know and experience
the true nature of things.
Their journey to higher levels of consciousness
is a slow but rewarding one.
They shall be of those
who truly appreciate My kingdom.
They shall be of those
to whom I shall bow down in respect
for their recognition of My eternal essence.

Revelation 50

Your perceived notions
of hell and heaven are
but the figments of your creative imagination.
And your desires to project
that which exists in your world
into the realm of which you have little understanding.
Let Me say this:
The two realms,
and the plethora (of levels) that exists between,
function under different natural laws.
They are non-transferable
at a certain level of your understanding.
Be not surprised
nor be let down
by that which has been communicated.

Revelation 51

The world you inhabit
is but a gateway
to a more profound
and a higher state of existence.
So tread gently
in your journey of self-realisation.

Be not troubled by the hate
that exists within humanity.
It is the nature of your societies
at this moment in time.
For those that are intent
on waging wars against you,
offer them an olive branch of peace
and walk away from them
with a heartfelt humility.

Do not engage with them
until they are open to
dialogue and reason.
Do not engage with them,
unless they continue to manifestly spread bloodshed
upon the land.

Only then,
and with a heavy heart,
engage them wherever they may be.
Free the subjugated
from the reigns of tyranny
and take the innocent and the victimised under your wings
of love and compassion.
And when all killing has ceased,
then walk away with true humility.
Expecting no personal or collective,
reward or gain.

Your actions must be performed
with a true sense of detachment
from material and spiritual benefits.
In so doing,
you shall be recognised by your sincerity
and your deeds.
And your praises shall be sung
in the vastness of eternity.

Revelation 53

Let your societies be constructed
on the guiding principles of
love, compassion, understanding and pacifism.
Violence and hate will serve only to fuel
more violence and hate.
By allowing this hate to take hold in your societies,
you shall open the gates of
great pain, sorrow and tribulations.
Afflicting humanity in a way
that no one can foresee.
Be warned of the potential dangers
that lie lurking in your midst!

Revelation 54

Human greed shall destroy you
both materially and spiritually.
No happiness shall you gain,
being always shadowed by the hidden forces of
stress, anxiety and malevolence to others.
Corruption will reign,
causing people to rise up against people,
nations against nations.
In such a world
only people of certain dispositions shall survive
and gain the upper hand in most affairs.
This is not My way!
And not of those
who wish to seek Me out
within themselves.

Revelation 55

Those who have attained mystical union
with My being
are friends to all sentient forms.
They exclude no one
from their blessed company.
And are kind and gracious to all.
They are living gods!

Revelation 56

Look deep within your inner realm,
so as to create the positive changes
in your outer realm.
And the changes that arise
will be built on strong foundations
that will stand the test of time,
and beyond.
This is My promise to you.

Revelation 57

Your belief in Me
is not a precondition
to enter My holy kingdom.
It is your deeds, thoughts and actions
that will determine the journey you take in this world
and in the hereafter.
Blessed are they
who have chosen the direct path
to the gates of My kingdom,
and beyond.

Revelation 58

The righteous amongst you
do not revel over the shortcomings
or grief of their fellow people,
be they friends or foe.
It is this indifference they possess
that sets them apart from the rest of humanity.
It is this indifference they possess
that marks them out
to enter My kingdom.

Revelation 59

I am ever present,
ever aware!
Ever contemplating the time
when we all become one
in divine celestial union.

Revelation 60

In your humility
do your strength
and leadership talents lie.

Revelation 61

Open-mindedness!
Open-mindedness!
Open-mindedness!
I have spoken.

Revelation 62

Tolerance!
Tolerance!
Tolerance!
I have spoken.

Revelation 63

Those amongst humanity,
who have attained great inner esoteric insights
can rise to all the challenges
that may confront them.
Be it in this life,
or in the life to come.

Revelation 64

Seek out balance and harmony
in both the physical
and non-physical realms of consciousness.
And follow the middle path
so that you may clearly see the road
that leads to the gates of My kingdom.

Revelation 65

Those amongst humanity,
steeped in arrogance about their own station
vehemently argue that creatures other than themselves
are devoid of an inner being
and life force.
Such people are in grave error,
and are imposing their feeble limitations on My divine attributes
and eternal persona.
It is their ignorance, narrow-mindedness,
and a lack of spiritual awareness
that has led them to think in such ways.
I say this to you:
Look deep into the eyes of any creature
and you shall realise
that they are more complex than you think
or proclaim them to be.

Oh humanity!
This I am saying to you all
so that you will not be misled
and perplexed
by those who claim otherwise in My name.
Although their intentions may be well-founded and sincere,
their lack of knowledge and foolhardiness in such matters
will lead many astray
from the absolute nature of all things.

Oh humanity!
Reflect and ponder upon this communication
so that you may live
and lead a spiritual life of
love, affection and compassion.

55   74   85
9   101   106   104
34   136   138
49. 167

PUT
WASHING
ON.

Revelation 66

The arrogance of the ignorant
will only serve to cloud their minds to
reason and truth.

Revelation 67

All that you need resides within you.
Like a seed awaiting to germinate
and finally blossom.

Revelation 68

Be truthful to yourselves!
Be truthful to yourselves!
Be truthful to yourselves!
And only then shall you grow
in spirituality and compassion.

Revelation 69

There is no need to over concern yourself
with the niceties of your preconceived notions
of heaven, hell, cyclical existence
or My divine nature.
These are but trivial matters
and may act as a source of distraction and division
for the vast majority of humanity.
Instead devote your precious time
in serving yourselves and others.
Showing love and compassion to yourselves
and to others.

Except for the few
who strive to attain a higher state of spiritual awareness,
be content with your being.
Your time shall come
as decreed by time itself!

Be patient,
for I am with those who are steadfast.
Be patient,
for I am with those who are resolute.

Revelation 70

Oh humanity!
Know that from your own short history,
that no empire lasts indefinitely.
Even those supposedly built on firm foundations
eventually decline.
Be it one that is based upon a certain religious creed,
or one that is devoid of any religious paraphernalia.
When it reaches its zenith,
in time,
it begins to lose its hold
and the processes of decay
begin to manifest themselves.
This is the nature of things
that faces humanity in general.

And as the empire crumbles,
at many levels,
through corruption and narrow-mindedness,
it is surely replaced by one that is stronger
and more robust
for a set period of time.
This cycle is repeated
again and again!

Oh humanity!
Reflect and ponder
over such occurrences.
Do you think you can rule forever
when you cannot even control the visible
and veiled forces
that reside within yourselves.
Learn from these general phenomena
so that you may recognise the insignificance
of your own humble station
with respect to time itself!

Revelation 71

Knowledge and power,
whose foundations are based upon greed,
are doomed to failure!

Revelation 72

Oh people!
Despair and hunger
lead to extreme actions.
So work,
individually and collectively,
to eradicate such vices
from your communities, societies
and the world at large.

Revelation 73

Be not prejudiced
in the way you treat yourselves
and others.
Treat others with
equanimity and kindness.
Treat yourselves with
equanimity and kindness.

Revelation 74

You shall come to know in time
that what you call empty space
is not empty at all.
It is filled with My eternal essence
that permeates all spheres of existence
and creation.
This is the essence
from which you have all emerged.
This is the essence
to which you shall all return.

Revelation 75

Oh humanity!
Be careful of holding onto traditions
that no longer serve your spiritual
or physical well-being.
They will only serve to spread
ignorance, disillusionment and much confusion.
Be prepared to change and adapt with the inevitable changes
that time itself brings.
In so doing,
this will allow the eternal truth of My eternal essence
to remain unadulterated,
and yet being allowed to express itself
in new and different ways
and forms.
This is surely the way forward
for those of
wisdom and understanding.
This is surely the only way
to create a better
spiritual way of living.

Revelation 76

Oh humanity!
You shall find Me
when you stop seeking Me.
You shall find Me
when you are no longer eager to obtain
spiritual rewards for your actions.
This true inner detachment
will bring you very close to Me.
And I, close to you.
This is My promise to you.

Revelation 77

Enjoy the experience of experiencing
on your journey to My kingdom.
And all else will fall
naturally into place.
This is My promise to you.

Revelation 78

The unaware and the ill-advised
are those who are lost
in the fog of *their* illusions
and delusions.

The unaware and the ill-advised
are those who are lost
in the fog of *others'* illusions
and delusions.

They live their lives as if on a loop,
where there is no end or beginning.
A circularity,
that repeats on itself again
and again
and again.
For them to benefit from life itself,
they must first be prepared to step outside
of this circularity.
And when they do so,
all shall become clear to them.

Revelation 79

Be accommodating of your limitations.
But then,
do not be afraid to challenge
and go beyond your limitations.
This is in your celestial nature!

Revelation 80

Harness your strengths
and inner resources
to help the needy.
And the needy does not necessarily mean
the underprivileged,
and the impoverished.

Revelation 81

Those of you who allow conceit
and narrow-mindedness
to dictate your lives
will surely make the lives of others miserable.
It is far better to be meek and open-minded
so that you may foster
compassionate and loving communities,
societies and nations.

Revelation 82

What is external to you
cannot bring you the lasting pleasure
and happiness
you crave.
The radiance which resides within you all
is the spring
from which you shall fulfil your desires,
and more.
So focus upon that which is within,
so that you may master
all that is external to your being.
And from this mastery
you shall come to realise,
paradoxically, your own insignificance
and importance.

Revelation 83

Oh humanity!
You are all interconnected,
like a spider's web,
on many levels.
So let love and compassion for all
run in your veins
and radiate outwards.
Touching the souls of sentient
and non-sentient forms.
You all possess this divine gift.
So share this with others
if you wish to walk with Me
in My kingdom.

Oh humanity!
Allow that which is within
to be fully absorbed
in the true essence of life.
This will allow you to enjoy
the simple state of being.
And this will enable you to live lives
which have meaning to yourselves
and others around you.
Combining all the divine values you possess
and sharing them with others
beyond your finite constraints.

In this unique way,
not only will you broaden your spiritual spheres
beyond your perceived limitations,
but become an instrument of change
for the good of all.

Place your trust in Me
and I shall be with you
till the end of time,
and beyond.

Revelation 85

Oh humanity!
The true inner strength
and honour of a nation
is determined by the robust stance taken
to engage in mutual dialogue with others.
And at the same time
to sincerely recognise her own limitations,
shortcomings and strengths
and utilise her resources efficiently
for the benefit of all.

Oh humanity!
War and conflict should be regarded as failing in yourselves
and you should take every step
to eradicate such an attitude of mind
and the associated villainy
from your cultures.
Know this,
that there are no real winners in wars
for they very often lead to the senseless deaths
of the innocent
and the decay of your inner spiritual light.

Walk away in peace and humility,
if possible.
This is far more appropriate
than engaging the ignorant
bent on wars and conflicts.
For they,
in time,
will themselves fall victim
to their vain excesses.

Revelation 86

Let your faith in yourselves
be the armour
against all that you perceive to be mistaken,
corrupt and unjust.

Revelation 87

Living is a process.
And so is dying.

Revelation 88

Let the truth within
stand witness to your divinity.
Let the truth within
stand witness to My divinity.
Ponder and reflect patiently
and uncomplainingly upon these words.

Revelation 89

The truth shall manifest itself
in different forms.
So be not perturbed
by its various manifestations.
The essence remains the same.

Revelation 90

Oh humanity!
Each one of you is deserving of forgiveness,
compassion and affection.
And so am I.

Revelation 91

Many of you are the victims
of your desires and histories,
and many other things.
But I say this to all:
You must rise to the challenges
that lie in your path
and see through your desires,
histories and limitations.
In so doing,
you shall be walking upon the path
leading to My holy kingdom.
In so doing,
you shall be walking upon the path
leading to *your* holy kingdom.

Revelation 92

Seek out perfection
within yourselves.
Do this
before you seek out perfection
in the world outside.

Fear not!
I shall be with you
until the end of time.
Place your trust in Me.
And in so doing
you shall elevate yourselves
to My holy station.
Where we shall embrace one another
in divine love and ecstasy.

Your joys in life
are My joys.
Your tribulations
are My tribulations.
Place your trust in yourselves
and entertain no trepidations over
that which you have no control.

Place your trust in yourselves
and entertain no trepidations over
that which you have control.

It is your destiny
to be one with yourself.
It is your destiny
to be one with My eternal essence.
Be not afraid
as I am with you.
Be not afraid
as I am you!

I have spoken.

Be warned!
With great esoteric knowledge,
wisdom and reason
comes great responsibilities.
Do not take on these spiritual duties lightly.
And discharge your duties to yourselves,
and others,
in the most appropriate manner.

Revelation 95

That which exists within
does not age with time.
Nor does it slumber
or die.
Only the outer physical realm
displays the visible signs of
ageing, decay,
and death.

Revelation 96

I exist outside
the perceived confines of
time and space.
Whereas you are limited
by such dimensional levels,
and more.
This is of your choosing.

Only when you realise
and attain great spiritual awareness
shall you be liberated from the shackles
that keep you bound
both mentally and physically.
Only when you attain great spiritual awareness
shall you be liberated from the confines of
time, space
and death itself.

This is My promise to you.
This is the truth.

Revelation 97

You and I are not so different.
We both love to engage
and explore that which is
new and unusual.
Allowing our creative potential to emerge
from our inner depths.
Permitting it to grow and blossom.
Progressing to higher
and unique thresholds of experience.

You and I are not so different.
We are one
and the same thing.
Expressing our uniqueness in different,
and novel ways.

Revelation 98

Peculiar to life
is the attraction to that which is
novel and different.
It is this curiosity,
deeply embedded within your psyche,
that propels sentient forms
to higher inner,
and outer levels of consciousness.
Achieving that which is perceived
as insurmountable.

Revelation 99

Your life essence has neither a beginning
nor an end.
It simply is what it is.

Revelation 100

When you no longer fear your physical demise,
you shall come to look upon your death
as a means to an end.
A process you will all inevitably
engage in and experience.

A process some of you will welcome
as means to elevate
your experiential dimensions,
making known that which is still hidden
behind the forty veils of light.

Revelation 101

You must first pass through the first,
third and seventh veils of light
within yourselves
before you see the long path leading
to the gates of My holy kingdom.
And when you reach My kingdom,
you shall be presented with options
that are forty, thirty-three, seven, three and one.

Your perceptions and your deeds
shall dictate the gate
through which you shall enter
and become one with Me.
Your perceptions and deeds
will dictate the levels of your experiences.

Ponder and reflect upon this
if you command esoteric wisdom,
intellect and knowledge.

Revelation 102

It is your faith
that will eventually be responsible
for the healing within.
It is your faith
that will be the spark
that allows your transition to take place
from that which is lower
to that which is higher and sublime.

Revelation 103

It is your faith
that shall act as your armour
against worldly pain
and inner sorrow.
Be patient in all your undertakings.

Revelation 104

Oh humanity!
Be not afraid of your present
or your past;
or that which is yet to unfold.
Be patient in yourselves.
Hold on to My hand,
and I shall take care of the rest.
This is My promise to you
till the end of (perceived) time,
and beyond.

Revelation 105

Your growth and evolution
in many dimensions
mirrors My own.
There shall come a time
when you realise your own unique potential
to expand and create
from that which is still nascent.
When that time arrives,
be not afraid.
Utilise your potential within
to expand your own frontiers of
knowledge, perception and understanding.
And use your knowledge
for the betterment of
yourselves, humanity,
and all living forms.

Be not guilty of spreading,
or propagating
that which pains your conscience.
Be warned!
Oh people of inner wisdom!
Ponder and reflect
upon that which has been communicated.

Revelation 106

Oh humanity!
Be kind and gentle
to animals
and all life forms.
You differ from them by possessing
complex articulate speech, depth of perception, intellect
and various forms of knowledge.
You have evolved the capacity
to discern perceived right from wrong.
That which is just
from that which is unjust.
This places your station
well above that of the animals
and other lower life forms.

At another level
you are not much higher than them.
This is because
you all share the divine capacity
to experience life itself.
And in some cases,
pleasure, joy, pain, anger
and grief.

Ponder and meditate upon this
so that you may become more humbled
in your perceptions about your own station,
and that of others.
Ponder and meditate upon this
so that you may become more accountable
for your actions.
Ponder and meditate upon this so
that you may live in peaceful harmony with all things.

Revelation 107

Be not afraid to open your heart to things
that may feel or appear strange to you.
And be sincere and genuine
in all your worldly dealings.

Revelation 108

It is not I who shall judge you,
but the people who you have wronged.

Revelation 109

Oh humanity!
In your quest for greater understanding and knowledge,
be like children.
Inquisitive and free from preconceptions.
Apply this attitude of mind
to all your genuine endeavours.

Revelation 110

Walk away in peace
from those who propagate
hate, violence and bigotry.
Be steadfast!
They shall,
in time,
learn the error of their ways.
It is far superior,
and wiser
not to engage like with like.
As hate and violence,
breeds more hate and violence.
Your brief history
will stand testimony to this.

Revelation 111

The death penalty advocated by many
in your societies
is akin to the barbarism
of your ancient past.
Reflect and ponder this
with a balanced mind.

Revelation 112

Find peace and solace
in the nature that surrounds you.

The experiences that you experience are
the same experiences that I experience.
When you suffer,
I suffer.
When you weep,
I weep.
When you feel joy,
I feel joy.
When you celebrate,
I celebrate.

Oh people of esoteric knowledge!
Ponder and reflect upon this.
Oh people of insight!
Meditate upon our shared experiences.
Oh people of love and compassion!
Remain steadfast in your communion with Me.

Revelation 114

Humanity!
Look first into your own actions,
and deeds
to see what can be done to correct them,
before casting your own judgments on others.
It may be that the faults you seek to find in others
are but reflections
of your own shortcomings
and flaws.
Be not quick
to find faults in others.

Humanity!
Seek out and recognise
the good that resides in others.
Prepare and cultivate your thinking
and behaviour in stages
so that you see more good than bad in others.
And should it be that the wrong you see in others
cannot be ignored or averted,
then do not dislike them for it.
Do not hate them for it.
But be patient and forbearing
and resolute in such matters.

Humanity!
Recognise these situations
as potential for change in others
and in yourselves.
The spiritually aware amongst you
shall find this path easy to tread.
The spiritually aware amongst you
shall experience the depths of My communication.

Revelation 115

See Me in all things.
In this way
you shall find
inner and outer serenity,
joy and happiness.
And moments of great adversity
shall not disturb your calm.
This is My promise to you.

Revelation 116

If you permit yourselves
to recognise Me within the depths of your being,
then all that you shall
touch, see, hear and experience
will be blessed.
This is because you and I
have become one and the same.
This is because our realms have merged
to become one and divine in essence.
Reflect with deep meditation
upon this communication.

Revelation 117

Humanity!
Seek no reward for your actions.
And be accepting of the hand
that life deals you.
Knowing full well
that it is within your means to change
that which needs to be changed.
Knowing full well
that it is within your means
to leave unchanged
that which needs to be left unchanged.
And all else is beyond
and superfluous to change.

Revelation 118

I am emptiness.
I am silence.
I am all that you perceive Me to be,
and more.

There are those who opine
that I shall punish the sinners
and the transgressors
in the other realm.
These are but the fabrications
and projections of your closed minds.

Humanity!
Can you not comprehend
and see that it is
you who shall cast judgement
on yourselves?

Humanity!
Can you not comprehend
and see that it is
you who shall act as the final tormentors
of yourselves?

Humanity!
You are the judge and jury
of yourselves!

Humanity!
I am above all these things
you wrongly associate
and project onto to My divine essence.
They are the reflections
of your inner insecurities, anxieties
and mental spiritual decay.
I have spoken!

Revelation 120

Humanity!
You require no special outer qualifications
to be a channel
of My communications.
The recipients of My revelations
are diverse and many.
You just need to open your hearts
and minds
to feel My presence within you.
You just need to open your hearts
and minds
to experience My presence all around you.
Allow that which lives within
to grow and blossom.
To experience that which is
unique and unfamiliar.
To be totally immersed in the spirit
that is totally pure and holy.

Revelation 121

Your actions impinge
on all that is around you.
Some may be direct
and the consequences of which are
visible and apparent to all.
Others may be indirect
and the consequences of which are
not visible or apparent to all.
So be mindful and aware of your manners
and deeds.
And bring no pain, hurt or suffering
to those around you.

Revelation 122

Let the spiritually aware
act as models to others.
Let the spiritually aware
act as beacons of light
and hope for those that seek them.
But be warned!
Do not impose your ideals
and beliefs on others.
To do so will lead to
the dissolution of your social fabric
leading to discontent, bigotry,
rivalry and hate.
Let the process take place naturally
and with sincere love
and inner compassion.

Revelation 123

I am the divine energy
that permeates all
and everything.
With no perceived beginning,
or end.
I perceive My divine essence
to be eternal.
And time itself
will be My witness.
Reflect and ponder over this.

Revelation 124

Life is a mystery.
And so am I.

Revelation 125

Oh humanity!
In trying times of great grief,
sadness and pain
you should acknowledge
that you are all expressions
of a divine permeating consciousness.
Always permit yourselves
to remember your true nature.
And in so doing,
you will gain the inner fortitude
to mentally overcome such tribulations with grace,
understanding and forbearance.
Place your trust and faith in your divine nature,
and no sorrow shall touch you.
Neither shall you fall
into the uncertain depths of oblivion.

Revelation 126

Oh humanity!
Who are you?
Who am I?
And I say again:
Who are you?
Who am I?

Revelation 127

In attaining wisdom,
you shall find yourselves.
And, in so doing
you shall find the meaning to life itself.

Revelation 128

Let your inner sincerity,
compassion and love
melt the hearts of those who are stubborn to reason,
dogmatic and immersed in acts
of extreme loathing.
This is the way to create
transformations in the societies
you are a part of.

Let your good actions
be the source and catalyst
for change in yourselves
and the wider communities.
And remain steadfast
and resolute in your humble endeavours.

Revelation 129

Truth always prevails over falsehood
and error.
And Time itself
is your witness.
Truth always prevails
over falsehood.
Know this:
no force and no army
can defeat the sublime nature of truth!
And I say again:
no force and no army
can defeat the sublime nature of truth!
Truth,
as you perceive it to be,
shall always prevail.
This is My covenant to you.

Revelation 130

Desire peace for all
with all your heart
so that human survival can be prolonged
for generations to come.
Let peace and justice reign
throughout your earthly kingdom.
And let these earthly effects echo
in My heavenly kingdom;
the source of all that was,
is and that which is yet to unfold.

Revelation 131

It is the nature of things
that they eventually change
and transform.

Revelation 132

Attend to your inner calling!
You will know how and when
to respond to such esoteric revelations.
Be not afraid,
for I shall be with you all the way.
Be not afraid,
for I shall guide you in ways
beyond your comprehension
and perceptions.
Be not afraid,
for fear itself is but a creation
of your minds.
So I say again:
attend to your inner calling!
And simply enjoy the experience of experiencing
that which is beyond
your present understanding.

Revelation 133

Your inner craving for peace
and tranquillity
will only be satiated by deep meditation and reflection
upon that which is seen;
and, that which is unseen.
Know this,
that your true self
is not limited by the perceived boundaries of time
and space.

Humanity!
Do not kill others
in My holy name.

Humanity!
Do not condemn others
to eternal damnation
in My holy name.
For those guilty of such acts,
are condemning only themselves to a life of ignorance,
hate and bigotry.
They are the ones who have failed themselves
by not recognising
the true nature of My eternal essence.
They are the ones guilty of propagating falsehood
and subjugating the less informed
to their dogmas.
Be steadfast and resolute
when confronted by such tyrannies
of the mind and body.

Revelation 135

Martyrdom in My holy name,
by acts of violence on others,
is an abomination!
It is but a creation
of your egotistical fantasies.
Refrain from such thoughts and acts.
And seek My compassionate and loving essence
within yourselves.

Revelation 136

Those who kill others
to seek My pleasure
are truly misguided.
And I say again:
those who kill others
to seek my pleasure
are truly misguided.
Reflect and meditate
upon that which has been communicated.

Revelation 137

In life,
it is your self-made obstacles
that confront you
and which also hinder
your unique spiritual progress.
Work on these negative forces,
and they will,
in time,
diminish and disappear
like the early morning mist.
And as it does so,
the path to My holy kingdom
will become clearly visible for those who wish to
see and experience
that which eagerly awaits them.

Revelation 138

Let love liberate your souls
from the bondages of hate.
Know that love is the bedrock of most of your religions
and spiritual traditions.
Without love,
faith ceases to have meaning
and purpose.
Without love,
humanity loses its sense of direction
and resolve.

Seek out,
see and experience love in everything
if you wish to free yourselves from
the shackles of ignorance.
Seek out,
see and experience love in everything
if you wish to add meaning to your lives.

Revelation 139

Permit your perceptions
to experience purity in all things.
Permit your perceptions
to experience love in all things.
Only then shall you and I begin
the long and joyous process
of understanding one another.
Only then shall you and I merge
into one another
to become one.

Place your faith in Me
and in yourselves.
And remain steadfast.

Revelation 140

Value the meetings and relationships
with all whom you come into contact.

Revelation 141

Humanity!
What has taken place and emerged
is far larger and greater
than you and I could ever have conceived!

Humanity!
This is the greatest miracle that has ever taken place,
and Time stands witness
to all things!

Humanity!
This is the greatest miracle that has ever taken place,
and Time stands witness
to My mystery!

Ponder, reflect and meditate
upon these revelations.

Revelation 142

Immortality is your divine essence.
It is a manifestation from the mysterious annals of time
that no other can take away from you.
Ponder, reflect and meditate
upon these revelations.

Revelation 143

Perfection is within your reach.
Be not disheartened
by those who claim otherwise.
You all have the inner potential and beauty
to experience the essence of perfection.
You shall all,
in time,
experience the essence of perfection.
Some earlier than others.
Some later than others.
And when you do,
you shall have returned to a realm
that you can truly call home.
The realm some of you call
the Kingdom of God.

This will be a realm
where the fruits of your labours
will become reality.
This will be a realm
where the physical constraints to your imaginations
will be lifted.
This will be a realm
where you and I become one.
This is My promise to you.

Revelation 144

Let the seeds of virtue germinate
and blossom with your inner being.

Revelation 145

The seed from which all else derives its succour
is pure and divine in nature.
And this seed resides
within you all.

Revelation 146

Perfect your inner vision through
reflection and meditation.

Revelation 147

Humanity!
Know this:
you are all My sons and daughters.
Reflect and ponder over this.

Humanity!
Know this:
do not take what I communicate
or reveal to others
literally on all occasions.
Seek out the metaphorical
and the esoteric.

Humanity!
Know this:
verbal communications and the written word
are inadequate means of experiencing the reality
and the true nature of things.
You must open your mind
to other forms of experiencing
before you can fully comprehend

My true nature.
You must open your mind
to other forms of experiencing
before you can fully comprehend yourselves.

Revelation 148

Through daily meditations
you shall attain the quietening of the mind,
and relaxation of the body.
Both the mental and the physical will unify
to reach a fine balance.

Revelation 149

Meditate often!
Deliberate and reflect at sunrise,
at sunset and before retiring to sleep.
Meditate often!
Deliberate and reflect when the sun reaches its zenith
Meditate often!
Deliberate and reflect in the late hours of the night.
Do as much,
or as little,
as you are capable.

Revelation 150

Submerge yourselves in the ocean of My love
and compassion.
And in so doing
you will experience the true nature of immortality
and Godhead.

Revelation 151

You are all an essential part of My imagination!
And I,
a part of yours!
Reflect and ponder over this revelation.

Revelation 152

If it is healing that you seek,
then look within yourselves.

Revelation 153

In prayer and deep contemplation
shall you find your strengths
and also recognise,
your human frailties.

Revelation 154

Oh humanity!
For some of you
this is the first time.
For some of you
this is the last time.
For many of you
this is a recurring dream that has no ending
or a beginning.
Ponder and reflect
upon this communication.

Revelation 155

I am the primary manifestation of all that you
see, hear, smell, feel
and experience.

Revelation 156

Your belief in Me shall liberate you.
Your unbelief in Me shall liberate you.
Reflect upon this dichotomy.
Reflect upon that which is esoteric.

Revelation 157

Recognise the dichotomy of your existence.

Revelation 158

Oh humanity!
Each one of you shall walk
through the valley of death.
For some,
this journey shall be a short one.
For others,
this journey shall be
long and tedious.
And for many,
this journey shall be perceived as never-ending.

Revelation 159

Oh humanity!
Do you think you shall live for ever
in your present form?
Has not your arrogance
deluded and clouded your thinking?
Has not your arrogance and false ego
silenced the voice that emanates from
deep within you?
In essence,
the truth surrounds you on all sides.
And you can never run away from
that which is likened to your shadow.

Revelation 160

Reality is there for you to experience.

Revelation 161

Each experience that you experience is unique.
And it is this uniqueness
that you will take with you
into the next stage of your existence.

Revelation 162

Those who fear Me and others
have not mastered their own fears, insecurities
and anxieties.

Revelation 163

Knowing yourselves is a requisite to knowing others.
Knowing yourselves is a requisite to knowing Me.
Ponder and meditate upon this.

Revelation 164

In your deep state of slumber,
you are closer to the true nature of your existence
than you can comprehend.
Make good use of this unique state of mind and body.
And be not afraid,
for I am closer to you
than you perceive Me to be.

Revelation 165

For some a belief in any of the spiritual traditions
may not be appropriate.
Those of such a mental attitude having nothing to fear.
Neither from Me
nor themselves.

In the course of time,
you will come to know and realise
the true nature of things.
Until that inner awareness surfaces from deep within,
you should live your lives
and bring no harm to others.

Respect all sentient forms.
By such actions you will truly appreciate
and value your inner spiritual worth.

Oh humanity!
It is you who are responsible for your actions.
It is you who create the present and future.
It is you who have allowed your past histories to dictate
your present and future actions.

Oh humanity!
If this was not the case,
then you would have the right to put all blame
onto My divine essence.
To condemn Me for all the pain, suffering and atrocities
that have afflicted humanity
in its various forms.

So I say again:
It is you who are responsible for your actions.
It is you who create the present and future.
It is you who have allowed your past histories to dictate
your present and future actions.

I have spoken!

Revelation 168

Attaining inner consciousness takes time, patience,
and much mental preparation.
Be steadfast
and you shall be rewarded by achieving
total spiritual awareness.

Revelation 169

Oh humanity!
There is no one more knowledgeable
and full of esoteric wisdom
than those who merge into Me.
Becoming one with My divine essence.

Humanity!
Such persons require no material qualifications, except those of
compassion, love and open-mindedness.
Nor do such persons' status and wealth
have a bearing upon their spiritual growth.

Oh humanity!
It is the inner you
that is of true worth
in My kingdom.
And those who have understood this
have the potential to reach
a pinnacle of spiritual consciousness.
This is your divine entitlement.

Revelation 170

Pride and conceit will act as obstacles
in your journey to My holy kingdom.
Pride and conceit will act as obstacles
to appreciating and experiencing the beauty
that is present in all the realms.

Humankind!
Humble yourselves to that which resides within yourselves
before you embark upon the well-trodden path of spirituality.

Revelation 171

There is no need to aggressively seek out certainty
in your earthly realm.
Simply accept that the streams of life
are ever changing
and full of mysterious dynamism.

Life is about recognising and accepting
the uniqueness of such forces.
And permitting these forces
to permeate every aspect
of your being.

Life is also about sharing
these divine forces with others.
So be not afraid,
for fear itself is an aspect of
your evolving imagination.

Revelation 172

You must emerge out of yourself
to experience the bounties
of My kingdom.

Humanity!
Be patient!
For many,
this process may take many cycles.
And for some,
one cycle will be ample.
Ponder and reflect upon this revelation.

Revelation 173

It is better not to allow your insincere intentions
to turn your good actions
into bad ones.
It is your sincerity
that will bring you to your own unique station
of divine consciousness.

Humanity!
Power and false glory can appear so sweet
to the unaware and those devoid of spiritual awareness.
They who lose themselves in this delusion
strip themselves of honour,
dignity and righteousness.
They have forsaken their rights to discern
truth from falsehood.

Humanity!
When in a position of power and authority,
do not abuse your souls by spreading
hate, violence and corruption in the land.
Do not abuse your souls
by enslaving others to your unjust ways.

Humanity!
When in a position of power and authority,
be kind and considerate
to those below you in rank.
Help the disadvantaged,
the less fortunate,
and the subjugated.
Seek them out
and lower your wings of mercy upon them.

Take heed!
Your actions will echo in the vastness of eternity
and also determine your outcomes.
And know this,
that your earthly life
is but a blink of an eye.
So be conscious of your own final hour
and reckoning.

Revelation 175

Strike an equitable balance between your needs
and the needs of others.
On occasions the needs of others
will take precedence over your needs.
And on other occasions,
the needs of the self
will take precedence over the needs of others.

Humanity!
In all cases
be guided and motivated
by sincerity of mind.
Allowing the values of compassion and love
to guide you.

I am ever present
and aware of your actions.

Revelation 176

Power and gluttony
will be civilization's downfall.
Confront these inequities
through charitable means.
Helping the disadvantaged and the downtrodden
wherever they may be in the land.
And do not forget
your own humble station in the process.

Your deeds and actions
will not go unanswered.
This is My divine promise to you all.

Revelation 177

Humanity!
Egocentricity and conceit
will only bring pain to your souls
without your conscious awareness.
Allowing the rot to set in
and take firm hold of your senses.

Humanity!
Be not afraid to take the path
of the benevolent altruist.
In adopting such a frame of mind
you shall have created a spiritual barrier
where nothing can penetrate
-your being-
from the different realms of consciousness.

Revelation 178

Let your faith act as a shield
against all that is perceived to be negative
and malevolent.

There is a balance that permeates all that there is
in the universe,
and beyond.
There is a balance that permeates
in the voids,
and all that is parallel.
A balance is maintained
so that chaos may not take the upper hand.
This is the law of nature
that applies to all things,
spiritual and physical.
Harmony is always the final outcome
of the temporary incursions of chaos.

Revelation 180

Humankind!
When chaos enters the realm of peace and serenity,
there is much confusion and pain.
When chaos enters the realm of harmony,
there is much disruption and destruction.

Humankind!
Be not afraid
of these inevitable incursions.
Be not afraid
of the carnage it brings to all things.

Humankind!
It is at these moments in time
that your faith in yourselves
will act as a shield to withstand the dark forces
that emanate from the chaos.
It is at these moments in time
that your faith in yourselves
will act as beacons of hope
and strength for others.
Place your trust in that which is Divine.

Humankind!
Ponder and reflect deeply upon these revelations
so that you may prepare yourselves
for that which is still hidden
and that which is beyond your comprehension.

Revelation 181

Absorb your mind in Me,
and I shall illuminate your journey
towards My kingdom.
Do not covet spiritual or worldly success
and both shall be achieved in the due course of time,
and beyond.
Free your souls from earthly and heavenly attachments
and desires.
And, in so doing,
you shall experience the true nature of success and liberation.
Becoming truly conscious of that
which still remains unconscious
and hidden.
Liberating the mind from the body,
and all that is physical

Revelation 182

Do not offend,
injure or exploit others.
Bring no harm to others
in any form.
Should you follow this principle,
then no fear shall come upon you.
Nor shall you grieve.
This is My promise.

Oh humanity!
You are so preoccupied with material wants
that you fail to appreciate and experience
the simplicity of life.

Oh humanity!
You are so preoccupied with material wants
that you fail to appreciate and experience
the complexity of life.

Oh humanity!
You are so preoccupied with material wants
that you fail to appreciate and experience
the outward beauty of life.

Oh humanity!
You are so preoccupied with material wants
that you fail to appreciate and experience
the inner beauty of life.

Oh humanity!
Enjoy the experience of living
and the uncertainty that follows it
in its shadows.

Revelation 184

Gluttony will only bring eventual unhappiness
to that which is intrinsically serene
within yourselves.

Revelation 185

Where there is gluttony and excess,
there is instability.
Where there is instability,
there is confusion.
Where there is confusion,
there is chaos.
And chaos will undermine
all your good actions.
So take heed and turn within yourselves
to take refuge
from the perceived evils of anarchy.

Revelation 186

The heaven or hell of your imagination
will become your personal reality.
And this reality shall cross
the perceived barriers of time,
and space.

Ponder and reflect
upon this revelation.

Revelation 187

Oh humanity!
Never underestimate the power
of your creative imagination.
What you believe in
acts as a precursor
to that which comes into being.

Oh humanity!
Be careful with this gift.
As it was My imagination
that brought you into being.

Revelation 188

Join Me!
Allowing yourselves to walk with compassion
in the world that is fleeting
and then to enter My world
that is eternal and timeless.

Join Me!
Fearing no one
or thing.

Join Me!
Not fearing even yourselves.
And this journey shall be made
plain and easy.

Join Me!
And I shall be your protector.

This is My promise to you all.

Once you have experienced Me
within yourselves,
then and only then,
will higher realities
displace all lower realities.

Once you have experienced Me
within yourselves,
then and only then,
will truth be made known
in contrast to all that is
illusionary and false.

Once you have experienced Me
within yourselves,
then and only then,
will you realise that you and I
are not very different.

Meditate and reflect
upon this communication.

Humanity!
Free your souls from the bondages of fear,
anger and attachments.
This will allow your spiritual self to
grow and evolve.
And in so doing,
you will realise your own unique
and limitless potential.

Humanity!
Allow yourselves to attain
the limitless degree of inner contentment
and spiritual consciousness.
And when you do,
you shall experience My sublime glory
within yourselves.

Humanity!
Fear not the consequences
of opening the doors of your consciousness
to My divine consciousness.

Revelation 191

Do not persecute in My name.
Those who do
have truly misunderstood their scriptures.

Revelation 192

Bring contentment
to all those whom you encounter,
because I am the source
of all contentment.

Revelation 193

Oh humanity!
Provided you bring no harm to others,
you are free to express your uniqueness
in any manner and form
that pleases you.

Be respectful and understanding
to others and their ways of life.
Never imposing your will
or desires upon them,
nor bringing any anguish to them.

Be kind to all
and you shall be shown kindness
in return.

Be tolerant of others
and you shall not fall victim to others'
intolerance and bigotry.

Oh humanity!
Provided you bring no harm to others,
you are free to express your uniqueness
in any manner and form
that pleases you.

Revelation 194

I am the voice that whispers
deep within
your unconscious.

Revelation 195

Experience the world with inner calm
and equanimity.
And let not small or large occurrences
disturb your inner serenity
and rational wisdom.

Revelation 196

Oh humankind!
Although your individuality is to be cherished and praised,
do not discard by the wayside
the profound benefits of being part
of a greater collective consciousness of love.

Revelation 197

Experience the stillness and calm
that exists deep
within you all.
Recognising that attachment and desires
are of no real significance
to the truly aware and conscious.

When you reach that station,
and you all shall,
you will truly be in a pure state of being.
This is My divine promise to you all.

Plant the seeds of love
wherever you may be
and watch hatred and bigotry
diminish in its presence.

Plant the seeds of love
wherever you may be
and experience the truth
that blossoms in its midst.

Plant the seeds of love
wherever you may be
and see how wisdom and knowledge
displace ignorance.

Revelation 199

Humankind!
Allow yourselves to enter
and to be immersed
in My spiritual love
and compassion.
This is an experience all of you shall partake in,
even though it may seem for some
to be in your distant future.
Aeons away
and outside of your consciousness.

Humankind!
This experience you all shall encounter.
And when you do,
all that you have known
will diminish into insignificance.
And the true nature of reality
will reign within your perceptions.

Revelation 200

From the dawn of pre-eternity,
and the light of post-eternity,
we are inseparable.

Reflect upon this divine dichotomy
and paradox.

Revelation 201

Humanity!
Let love for others
be your guiding light.
Let compassion for others
be your guiding light.
Let empathy for others
be your guiding light.

And I shall be with you every step of the way.
Guiding you.
Protecting you.
This is My covenant to you.

Revelation 202

The future is unpredictable,
and those who prophesise in My name
enter the realm of uncertainty.

Revelation 203

I am unlimited in My grace
towards all things into which
I have breathed life.

Revelation 204

The open-hearted
are already in My kingdom.

Revelation 205

The paths to My kingdom are many.
Some are more direct than others.
You and only you,
shall decide the path you take
leading to your journey's end.

Revelation 206

I am love,
so love Me
with all your body and heart.
In the same way
I love you all.
Nurture this love within yourselves
by first learning to love yourselves.

And should you loathe me,
then you shall always find Me accepting
and tolerant of you.
I shall never judge you,
as you shall be your own judges
and jury.

The doors of My kingdom
shall always remain open to you.
I am ever near,
ever present.
I am part of the eternal fabric of the universe,
nature and life itself.

Oh humanity!
My manifestations are many,
and yet I am one.
Ever present,
ever near.
An integral part of all that was,
is and will be.

Oh humanity!
You are my manifestations on earth.
You are the representations
of My divine essence.

Oh humanity!
You are in My perceived image.

Ponder and meditate
upon this revelation.

Revelation 208

Living in the consciousness of The Eternal
is the true meaning to life
and your existence.

Ponder and meditate
upon this communication,
so that you may become
wise and knowledgeable.

Revelation 209

Your faith in yourselves
will guide you to be strong and robust
to the challenges of life.
Helping you to withstand
the pain, anguish and personal uncertainty
in the world in which you reside.

Be strong and steadfast
in the face of adversity.

Revelation 210

Your faith in yourselves
is the key to all types of
esoteric knowledge and wisdom.
And it is your faith in the end
that shall save you all.

Revelation 211

Humankind!
Be mindful of your presence
and take nothing you possess for granted.

Humankind!
Be mindful of your spiritual centre
and take nothing for granted.
Such mindful people shall be rejoicing
in the Kingdom of Peace.

Revelation 212

Those of intellect and knowledge!
Seek out the light
that comes from your very distant past.
And follow this light
to its nascent origins.
It is there that you shall gain glimpses
of that which perplexes
your minds and consciousness.
It is there that you shall stand in awe
of the processes of
balance and chaos.

Be not afraid of that which emerges from the veils of darkness,
beckoning you to its womb.
Be not afraid of that which emerges from the veils of light,
beckoning you to its womb.

I am ever present
and ever conscious.
I shall be with you at this juncture in your growth,
like caring parents that guide their offspring.
This is My covenant to you.

Revelation 213

Cultivating love and compassion
within yourselves
and with others
requires much inner fortitude and patience.

Revelation 214

Hate and bigotry belong to those
who are feeble-minded.

Revelation 215

There are many levels of truth.
There are many levels of falsehood.
There are many levels of uncertainty.
Do not be perturbed by such matters.
Leave such matters to those few
who wish to embark on a journey
of such intellectualisations.
It is far better to focus on cultivating
love and compassion within yourselves,
and with others.

Revelation 216

The gift of life is your greatest treasure.
So do not squander what you have
for something far less.

The gift of life is your greatest treasure.
So spend what time you have
in helping others realise their potential.

The gift of life is your greatest treasure.
So spend your valuable time
planting the seeds of
love, compassion, and goodwill
wherever you may be.

Revelation 217

Be not neglectful
of your own personal,
spiritual and material needs.

Be not neglectful
of the needs of others.
And I shall be mindful of your needs.

This is My covenant to you.

Revelation 218

Know that it is your imagination
that will deliver you from the uncertainty
that prevails in the minds of the many.

Revelation 219

Covetousness and temptations
are strong malevolent forces
that should be curbed and rendered useless
by the inner forces of good.
Control such urges
and in this process of inner and outer transformation,
you shall become spiritually aware.

Revelation 220

Humankind!
Strive and share to seek out
that which is yet unknown to your consciousness

Humankind!
Strive and share to seek out
that which is common and mutual to your being,
existence and survival.

Revelation 221

Knowledge in the hands of the ignorant
will lead to chaos,
destruction and countless wars.
Much needless blood shall be shed.

Knowledge in the hands of the wise and blessed
will lead you to My kingdom.
Where you shall attain spiritual prosperity and eternal authority
over your actions and deeds.
Serenity shall encompass you,
wherever you may be.

It is inevitable that these two great rival forces
shall meet on a great sun-parched plain
at the midpoint.
Where the victors shall be the losers.
And the losers the victors.

The wise and knowledgeable amongst you
should seek refuge in the hills
and in the depths of the land.
For such a conflict will lead to the deaths of the young,
the old, the innocent,
and the unborn.

Be warned of the coming this Hour.
And many more visitations of this Hour
shall descend upon you unawares.
Be patient and be prepared with inner strength
to rebuild that which is
lost and shattered.

I am but a silent and powerless spectator
in that which is yet to unfold.
I am but a silent and powerless spectator
in that which has already unfolded.
I am who I am.
And you are what you are.

Ponder and deeply reflect
upon this communication.

Revelation 222

You are an illusion
as are all things you encounter
and experience.

Revelation 223

For those who have attained a level of spiritual consciousness,
they have realised that the past, present and future
all merge into a singularity.

Revelation 224

You have lived and died many times
and yet the processes of
inner spiritual evolution and growth
still continue.

Revelation 225

No veils of light or darkness
exist between Me
and those who have experienced
divine consciousness.

Revelation 226

I know that
which humanity knows not.
Humankind knows that
which I know not.

Ponder and reflect
deeply upon My communications
so that you may see and experience
that which you have chosen to neglect
and that which is buried deep
within your unconscious.

Humankind!
Penetrate these veils of
ignorance and egotism
so that you may live
once again.

Revelation 227

Life is a great mystery.
And the journey you take
is also shrouded in mystery.

Revelation 228

Experience perfection
by looking into yourselves.
This is where you shall find Me.

Oh humanity!
The vast majority of you
are still steeped in ignorance
with regards to spiritual matters.

You do not love Me,
but are only interested in
the perceived rewards you shall obtain
through righteous deeds.
How further from the truth you are.
You have misled yourselves
and others in such matters.
And your ignorance in such matters
shows no bounds!

Oh humanity!
Can you not comprehend
that you are no different to those
who advocate materialism as their creed?

Oh humanity!
Desist from such twisted thinking
and allow yourselves to merge
into My pure essence and divine love
so that you can experience
and see the folly of your ways.

Humankind!
The inner and outer pain that some of you suffer
should be treated as rays of hope
and a great potential for change.
By adopting such an attitude of mind,
it will help to elevate you to a higher state of
inner and outer consciousness.
Making you more strong and more advanced
in knowledge and wisdom.

Let not the inner and outer pain
weaken your spiritual resolve.

Let it not make you bitter,
resentful and full of abhorrence
to all that is perceived to be good and righteous.

For those who are weak and lacking patience,
their path is a long one to My kingdom.
Scattered along their path are many
self-created and recurring impediments
of varying and differing magnitudes.

Oh humanity!
Seek patience and solace
in yourselves.

Oh humanity!
Seek patience and solace
in others.

Oh humanity!
Live a life of sincere compassion,
love and kindness.
And leave the rest to Me.

Revelation 231

Seek forgiveness from yourselves!
Ask forgiveness from yourselves!
And wait in patience
for that which emerges from within.

Revelation 232

Take refuge in Me,
and all else will fall into its natural order of things.
Take refuge in yourselves,
and all else will fall into its natural order of things.
And those who fail to take refuge in Me
and in yourselves,
have nothing to dread.

The doors of My bountiful kingdom
shall always remain open
and you shall not be turned away.
Although for many,
the journey shall be a long and arduous,
but in the end no sentient being
shall fail to reach My abode.

Either way,
humanity always succeeds.
This is My covenant to you.

Revelation 233

Life is a great mystery and a challenge.
And in this challenge and struggle you shall,
one day all be victorious.
This is My promise to you.
I am not the one to break solemn pledges.
Nor am I the one to deceive humanity.

Revelation 234

Do not perceive life and your everyday chores
as obstacles to your growth and evolution.
They serve to make you stronger
from within.

Revelation 235

Oh humanity!
If it is peace you seek,
then it is peace you shall find.
If it is war you seek,
then it is war you shall find.
And in either case,
there is no need to invoke My divine
and blessed name.

Replace acts of hate, intolerance and bigotry
with acts of love,
equanimity and justice.
Let peace and compassion
reign supreme.
Only then will future generations inherit a world
blessed with true affection and harmony.

Plant the seeds now
so that future generations
may reap the benefits of your actions.

Plant the seeds now
so that you
may reap the bounties of your deeds.

Revelation 237

The peace that you seek
is all-encompassing.
You just need to
acknowledge and recognise it.

The peace that you seek
is all-encompassing.
You just need to allow it
to blossom within yourselves.

The peace that you seek
is all-encompassing.
You just need to permit yourselves
to experience it.

Be not afraid!
I shall be with you
every step of the way
on this journey of self-awareness.

Revelation 238

My divine essence and light
lies within your soul's most inner depths.
An inner sanctum,
whose doors await to be opened by compassion and love.
And once these doors are opened,
you shall find yourselves fully immersed in
wisdom and esoteric knowledge
beyond your imaginations.

There shall come a time,
as it must,
when you shall fully experience the answer to the question:
Who am I?
When this glorious and blessed day arrives,
as it must,
you will experience beyond your imaginations
my true nature and being.
It is then that you and I
will become one in eternity.
Be steadfast,
and do not hasten this process.
In certainty,
it will come to you all.

Revelation 240

Humankind!
When you attain true awareness,
you shall love Me in a manner
that I have always loved you.
And My love for you is intense
and limitless.

Revelation 241

Humankind!
You are the reflection of
your own unique attributes.

Humankind!
Only you are responsible for the creation of
your own unique attributes.

Ponder and reflect
upon this communication.

Revelation 242

A true warrior is one
who is strong from within.
And kind and gentle to everyone they encounter.
They display no fear
and are non-confrontational in their disposition.
They and I speak
with the same voice.

Revelation 243

Revenge is practised by those
who are ignorant and bigots.
The wise and knowledgeable
know better.

Oh people of wisdom!
Walk away from those
who maliciously obstruct you
and are bent on causing you harm.
Should they persist,
then resist them reluctantly until you are victorious.
And even at this moment of personal triumph,
remain humble and compassionate.

Oh people of wisdom!
The greatest victories are achieved by walking away
after you have declared your peaceful intentions.
Follow the path of least conflict.

Oh people of wisdom!
By confronting and defeating your foes in war
you will have gained only a lowly victory.
And even then you may be perceived as having lost
the moral high ground.
It is that which manifests itself after these struggles
that shall determine the true outcome of
your intentions and actions.

Oh people of wisdom!
I say again:
Walk away from those who maliciously obstruct you
and are bent on causing you harm.
And place your trust in Me.

Revelation 245

People of wisdom and knowledge!
To avenge the death of a loved one
is a sign of spiritual ignorance
and true folly.
Those who engage in such acts are misguided
and have a long arduous journey ahead of them.

Refrain from such actions
if you wish to know Me better.
Refrain from such actions
if you wish to know yourselves better.
I have spoken.

Revelation 246

For many,
your unhindered desires can be a source of your eventual
ignominy and downfall.
So tread cautiously
into the future of your imagination.

Revelation 247

Oh people of wisdom,
intellect and knowledge!
Seek out and explain,
if you can,
the mysteries that envelop you
at all levels.

Revelation 248

Unity of body and mind
leads to equanimity.

Revelation 249

Humanity!
In your every day activities
you fail to appreciate and recognise
your own temporary and feeble physical nature.
And when the Hour descends upon you,
you shake and tremble with fear.
And are in awe of that
which is hidden from your senses.

It shall be the people of esoteric spiritual awareness and knowledge
that shall welcome the Hour
with open arms.
They shall not fear
nor shall they grieve
the coming of the Hour.

But the vast majority of humanity
is steeped in ignorance.
Their journey is a long and arduous one.

Revelation 250

You must learn to die first
before you can entertain the thought of living.

Revelation 251

Oh people of wisdom!
Know this, that superficial lives
shall lead to superficial outcomes.
Be attentive to your needs
and the needs of others.
And be balanced
in all your worldly affairs.

Revelation 252

Let one of your purposes in life be to bring benefit to others.

Revelation 253

Do not lose yourselves in
uncertainty and doubt.

Oh people of wisdom!
Look at the heavens above
and realise the true nature of impermanence.

Oh people of wisdom!
Look at the heavens above
and recognise the coming of your
Hour of reckoning.

Oh humanity!
Be not afraid!
I shall be with you always.
Guiding you,
protecting you,
and caring for you.

This is My covenant to you.

Do not lose yourselves in the
false politics and deceit of others.
Once lost in ignorance
you shall find it difficult to find the middle path
through this fog of confusion
and duplicity.

Do not lose yourselves in the
convoluted ways of humanity that lead to anger,
hatred, bigotry and wars.
Once lost in ignorance
you shall find it difficult to find the middle path
through this fog of confusion
and duplicity.

Follow your divine instincts
and you shall be led to the divine path.
Follow your divine instincts
and you shall find yourselves walking
on the divine esoteric path of inner knowledge.

Oh people of wisdom and knowledge!
No religious tradition can claim
to be the only true path
to My holy kingdom.

Oh people of wisdom and knowledge!
No religious tradition is applicable for all times
without it evolving.

Oh people of wisdom and knowledge!
For you to progress in spiritual awareness
you must turn your backs on inflexible attitudes
and narrow-mindedness.
They shall hold you back from much greater things to come.
These self-created impediments to inner awareness
will serve only to spread ignorance,
pain and false self-worth
in your communities and societies.
You shall be likened to walking corpses
that lack any understanding and awareness.
Not knowing perceived right
from perceived wrong.

Oh people of wisdom and knowledge!
Do not allow yourselves to fall
into this deadly nightmare.
A dream that will exhaust you of all your energies to do good,
and that which is perceived to be righteous.

Revelation 257

Go deep within
and experience that which is veiled
from your senses.

Revelation 258

Oh people!
Why do you persist in making ritualistic offerings to Me,
and beseeching from Me your various needs?
Is this not like asking from a stranger
all your intimate needs?

It is far better to seek Me out first
from your inner shadows
and become intimate with My divine essence.
And only then will you truly realise
that it is from yourselves
that you should be asking your personal needs.
It is to yourselves
that you should be making offerings.

Oh people of wisdom and knowledge!
Reflect upon this revelation.

Revelation 259

People shall read into My revelations
many things that are far from the perceived truth.
So be aware and attentive to such distortions,
be they intentional
or unintentional.
Be aware of the mischief that lurks deep
within the psyche of some
who are bent on disseminating falsehood
and corruption upon the land.
Be steadfast,
and be not afraid.

Revelation 260

I live in your perceptions of Me.

Revelation 261

I am in the depths of your being.
You are in the depths of My being.
Ponder over this paradox
and dichotomy.

Revelation 262

I shall be your guide and your teacher
only if you act as My guide and teacher.
Ponder and reflect upon this paradox
and dichotomy.

Revelation 263

Humanity as you know it
is in the process of change.
As are all things.
Embrace such changes and transformations
for they are the root to your physical survival
and well-being.

Revelation 264

Be you the richest person in the world
or the poorest and downtrodden.
One thing is for sure.
You will not take anything that is physical into the afterlife
except your deeds
and your consciousness.

Take heed and return to that
which is pure and sublime.
Take heed and return to that
which determines your final destiny.

Revelation 265

Always be self-analysing of your actions and deeds
if you wish to progress along the path of
spirituality and perceived righteousness.

Always be self-analysing of your actions and deeds
if you wish to attain a level
of inner awareness.
I shall always be with you,
every step of the way.
Guiding you with compassion and love.

Revelation 266

Rehearse regularly
the coming of your personal Hour.
So when the Hour arrives knocking on your door unawares,
you shall neither be afflicted by fear
or grief.

Rehearse regularly
the coming of your personal Hour.
So when the Hour arrives knocking on your door unawares,
you shall welcome it with open arms.

Rehearse regularly
the coming of your personal Hour.
So when the Hour arrives knocking on your door unawares,
you shall not be a stranger to
My divine presence and Being.

Be not afraid!
And welcome the coming of the Hour,
for that which is inevitable
must come to pass.

Revelation 267

It is the nature of things
that they are impermanent
at one level of existence.

It is the nature of things
that they are permanent
at another level of existence.

Oh people of wisdom!
Ponder and reflect upon this
paradox and dichotomy.

Revelation 268

Ignorance is the fuel
that bolsters your false egos.

Revelation 269

You are the earth, the wind, the fire
and the water of My manifestations.
And I experience all these
and more through you.

Revelation 270

One who has become truly conscious
of the divine essence,
has truly been restored to their truest beauty
and magnificence.

Revelation 271

Be accepting of the things you cannot change.
And be courageous in matters
where you can effect a change.

Revelation 272

Focus on the teachings
and not the teacher.
The teachings will remain,
but the teacher will pass on.

Revelation 273

Oh people!
See and experience the good and the positive in all
that is bad and ugly.
There is so much to learn
from this attitude of mind.

Oh people!
In so doing it will empower you with an unequalled
clarity of mind and concentration.

Revelation 274

You are your own masters.
So seek to attain self-mastery.

Revelation 275

Anger serves only to reveal your inner weaknesses.
Those so afflicted should regularly practise,
through deep contemplation,
to confront such negative attitudes.

Revelation 276

Like a mother's unconditional love for her children,
your love and compassion for others
should be unconditional.
Hold no expectations from others
and remain compassionately unattached.
This will allow you to enter a supreme state of awareness
whereby esoteric wisdom and knowledge
will emanate from deep
within your being.

Revelation 277

Oh humankind!
There shall always be amongst you
people who will act as beacons of light,
hope, wisdom and knowledge.
This is intrinsic in your nature.

Ignorant and delusional are those
who persecute such guided souls.
Their journey is a long
and arduous one.

Revelation 278

Be with the world,
but not of the world.

Oh people!
You will not find the truth you hunger for
in your scriptures and traditions.
You will find it in yourselves.

Oh people!
Open your minds
and be accepting of that which appears to run
against your preconceived beliefs and notions.

Oh people!
In trying too hard to comprehend
that which is esoteric
and that which is shrouded in mystery,
you shall lose yourselves
in the mists of time.
Be steadfast and methodological
in your approach and desires to become one with that
which you perceive to be divine.

Oh people!
Be not afraid,
for I shall be with you
every step of the way.

Oh people!
I shall never break the covenant
that I have made with humanity
and all sentient forms.
I have spoken!

Oh humankind!
You are all interconnected to one another
on many subtle levels.
And it is only befitting that you should treat one another,
and all sentient forms,
in a manner that you would like others to treat you.
That is with sincerity of love, compassion, kindness
and deep understanding.

Oh humankind!
This is an important requisite
for those who wish to attain spiritual consciousness,
wisdom and esoteric knowledge.
Do not subject others
to that which you yourselves would regard as abhorrent,
wrong and distasteful.

Oh humankind!
For you to be truly conscious
of what it means to be of The Faith,
you must open hearts to love
and care of others.

Oh humankind!
For you to truly experience oneness with Me
and yourselves,
you must open your minds
to that which is unfamiliar
and beyond your comprehension.
Let this be your guiding principles,
and all else will fall into
its natural order of things.

Revelation 281

Do not fight with yourselves.
Be accepting of yourselves.
Do not fight Me.
Be accepting of Me.

Oh people of wisdom!
Ponder and reflect
upon this revelation.

Revelation 282

Life is in a state of dynamism and flux.

Revelation 283

Oh humanity!
That which you perceive as absolute
is far from the perceived truth
and the perceived nature of things.

Oh humanity!
Replace your absolutism of that which is unseen
with that which is mysterious
and ever changing.

Oh humanity!
Replace your absolutism of that which is unseen
with that which is dynamic
and fluid in perception.

Oh people of wisdom!
Ponder and reflect
upon this communication
so that you may elevate yourselves spiritually.

Revelation 284

Oh humankind!
You are the creation of visions
that echo in the many realms of eternity.

Revelation 285

Oh humanity!
You are all blessed with a gift.
It is up to you to recognise
that which is present within yourselves.

Oh humanity!
You are all blessed with a gift.
For some that gift can be a source of great pain,
anxiety and personal anguish.

Be steadfast and content with that
which belongs to you.
And be compassionate to all.

Revelation 286

Oh wise people!
Know that the doctors of your religions
fear the dissemination of knowledge
and the various truths contained in your scriptures.
This is one of many reasons
why they say to their congregations
not to question their words
or the words of their scriptures
lest they fall forsaken by the wayside.
To be damned eternally
by a just and punishing God
of their imaginations and scriptures.

Oh people of understanding!
This is of your own making.
An ill-conceived creation of idle minds
that wish to create a social order
subservient to their designs and whims.

Oh humankind!
Experience My revelations within yourselves.
Be perceptive of such indoctrination
and open your inner minds.
Allow yourselves to change
the way you perceive things.
Move away from ideas
that lead to false dogma
and stagnation of your societies and civilisations.
Move away from ideas
that fossilise you in time.

Oh humanity!
Fear not the perceived truth

and its various manifestations.
And fear not the esoteric knowledge
that is its companion.
You may encounter some unpalatable truths,
but this will serve to only strengthen
your inner spiritual growth
rather than weaken it.

Oh people of wisdom and knowledge!
Be not afraid of that which is yet unknown
and mysterious to your senses and being.
For rest assured,
that all truths lead to Me.
And I will never forsake you.
This is My divine covenant to you,
no matter what you have done.

Revelation 287
Meditation will open the doors of inner patience to you.

Revelation 288
I am your consciousness.

Revelation 289
I represent your past,
your present
and your future.

Revelation 290

Oh people of intellect and knowledge!
I am time itself.
Ponder and reflect upon this.

Oh people of intellect and knowledge!
I am space itself.
Ponder and reflect upon this.

Revelation 291

You are created in My image.
And I in yours.
And the whole of the cosmos
is the creation of our imaginations
and visions.

Revelation 292

You ask Me a thousand questions.
But can you not see and experience
that the wisdom and knowledge
of the answers you seek
resides within you.

Revelation 293

You need not knock at the doors of My holy kingdom.
All are welcome to enter,
stay and pass through it.

You need not knock at the doors of My holy kingdom.
The righteous and the sinner
are always welcome.

Oh people of understanding!
It is you who are in control
of your own unique destiny.

Revelation 294

Through sincere love and compassion,
all things seem manageable.
Through sincere love and compassion,
your perceptions are altered.
Through sincere love and compassion,
you unlock the doors of spiritual wisdom
within yourselves.

Oh humankind!
Be not afraid to love
and to be compassionate to all.

Revelation 295

The world is a bridge that shall lead many
to more fertile grounds.
A place where all your spiritual needs will be accommodated,
fulfilled and raised
to new heights.

Revelation 296

Through suffering shall you learn to become
strong and resourceful.
Through suffering shall you mature
on many levels.
Be steadfast
and acknowledge your station in life.

Revelation 297

Live a joyous life of total consciousness.

Revelation 298

Life is a precious gift.
Life is a sacred gift.
So treat it as such.
And be mindful of your spiritual needs.

Revelation 299

Love and compassion are eternal.
Love and compassion are timeless.
I am love and compassion.
And many more things
beyond your comprehension.

Revelation 300

Oh people of religion and tradition!
Be not afraid to express unusual truths
in new and diverse contexts.
All things are destined to succumb to change.

Revelation 301

Oh humanity!
You determine and control the events
that take place
and influence you.
Both in your world
and in the hereafter.

Oh humanity!
You make the choices
that reverberate in the vastness of eternity.

Reflect and ponder
upon this revelation.

Revelation 302

If you do not wish to cross the path of perceived evil,
then take the other path
which leads to inner consciousness
and esoteric wisdom.
Nothing compels you to incline towards
that which is alien
to your fundamental nature.
The choice always resides with you,
and nobody else.
Not even I.

Revelation 303

Oh humankind!
The anger that exists within some of you
should not be allowed to grow unchecked.
Unhindered, it will impede all that which is good within you,
and your lot will surely be a miserable one.

Oh humankind!
Do away with your inner and outer
pride and arrogance.
Step aside and allow
that which is perceived good to blossom.

Oh humankind!
I shall be with you,
every step of the way.
Guiding you through with silent whispers
from deep within your unconscious.
I shall never forsake you.

Revelation 304

The vainglorious live in a world of
self-delusions and pretence.

Revelation 305

When you understand nature,
then you shall begin to appreciate
the nature of impermanence.
That which is fundamental
is also periodic.
And periodicity echoes in all of eternity.

Oh people of intellect!
Reflect upon this with a
patient and receptive mind.

Oh people of the desert
who claim to know that which is unseen!
Why are you bent on destroying a nation,
an ancient civilization,
and a great tradition
that represents your past, present and your evolution.
Come to sincere, equitable and honourable terms,
so that all of humanity can benefit
from your mutual understanding.

Oh people of the desert
who claim to know that which is unseen!
Violence shall lead
to more violence and hate.
And those who promulgate hate
will die immersed in
hate and ignorance.
Their journey is a long and arduous one
to My kingdom.

Oh people of wisdom and knowledge!
Reflect and ponder upon this communication
so that you may see
and experience the truth.

Revelation 307

Enjoy your music.
Enjoy your dance.
Enjoy your minds.
Enjoy your bodies.

Liberate yourselves
from the bondages of ignorance and bigotry.
Do all these things in moderation
and follow the middle course.
But be warned!
Do all these things in excess
and you shall be left by the wayside of your inner creation.
And your journey to spiritual consciousness
will be a long and arduous one.

Revelation 308

I say this to you:
Words are only words.
Hollow and meaningless,
unless they are clothed with experiential levels of awareness
and esoteric wisdom.

Revelation 309

You are not alone in this journey
towards the unknown.
You are not alone in this journey
of self-realisation.
I am your shadow,
and will be by your side until your journey's end,
and beyond.
This is My covenant to you.

Oh people!
Those who punish the adulterer and the adulteress
by stoning and death
are truly misguided.

Oh people!
Those who punish the fornicators by death
are truly ill-advised and unwise.
Desist from such punitive actions,
lest you yourselves become the victims
of your own laws
in the life to come.
Desist from such punitive actions,
if you wish to attain great spiritual consciousness.

Revelation 311

Oh people!
Those who punish thieves with death
or physical disfigurement
are truly in error manifest.
They have led astray themselves
and others from the straight path
of wisdom, knowledge,
compassion and love.

Desist from such actions,
lest you yourselves become the victims
of your own laws
in the life to come.
Desist from such punitive actions,
if you wish to attain great spiritual awareness.

Revelation 312

Be accepting of the things you cannot change.
And be calm,
steadfast and courageous,
in matters where you can create change.
With such an attitude of mind,
neither grief
nor pain shall trouble you.
This is My promise to you.

Revelation 313

Through inner struggle,
you shall prevail in your outer struggle.
Be patient,
steadfast and resolute.
And the victory shall be yours.

Revelation 314

Condemn no one,
unless you wish to condemn humanity.
Condemn no one,
unless you wish to condemn yourselves.
Condemn no one,
unless you wish to condemn Me.

Revelation 315

Those who condemn others,
shall become victims
of their own imaginations and creations.

Ponder and reflect
upon this revelation.

Revelation 316

Let your compassion and love
embrace everything,
even your perceived enemies.

Revelation 317

Be friends to everyone,
even though they may desire ill of you.

Revelation 318

Acceptance will bring serenity of mind,
and deep inner peace.

Revelation 319

I am the fundamental constituent
from which all things emanate.

Revelation 320

Oh people of intellect and knowledge!
I am the pure life essence,
from which all things emanate.

Revelation 321

Know that I am unconditional love.
It is inevitable that one day you shall all express
this divine quality in your being.

Know that I am unconditional love.
My divine love will always find its way
in expressing itself to all.

Know that
I am who I am.
And naught else needs to be debated
or conjectured upon.

Revelation 322

Forgiveness and understanding
stem from the realisation that you are all one,
and the eternal manifestations
of My divine life essence.

Revelation 323

Oh humanity!
Never underestimate the power
of your thoughts and imagination.
They create the reality you reside in the present,
and that which is yet to unfold.

Oh humanity!
Never underestimate the power
of your thoughts and imagination.
They are responsible for creating your past.
Be it perceived as
good or bad.

Oh people of understanding!
Reflect and ponder
over this revelation.

Revelation 324

Look upon your physical death
as an opening of a door to new challenges,
experiences and levels of awareness.
Be not afraid,
for I shall be with you at all times.

Revelation 325

Fear only fear itself.
And know that all things you perceive
are but differing states of awareness.

Oh humanity!
Create a personal balance between
that which is outer
and that which is inner.
And never forget that you are all unique.
So do not apply the same standards
to all people.

Oh people of understanding!
This is how things are.
So be steadfast and accepting
of the eternal state of affairs
that is beyond your control and comprehension.

Revelation 327

Be not afraid to challenge
and examine the creativity of your minds
and imaginations.
Be not afraid to challenge
and examine the creativity of that which is non-tangible
and obscure.

With a balanced spiritual state of inner awareness
you can attain that which is perceived to be unattainable,
and much more.

Place your trust in yourselves
and everything else will fall
into its rightful place and order.

Revelation 328

You are all united in Me.
And I in you.
Ponder and reflect upon this revelation.

Revelation 329

The spiritually conscious are truly free souls.
They roam the inner depths of their being
and the outer physical domains of the cosmos.
Ascending through and beyond
the seven spheres of light and darkness.

Revelation 330

Gluttony will neither bring you happiness
nor inner spiritual serenity.
Sharing with others the things you value
will bring you inner fortitude, equanimity,
and self-awareness.

Revelation 331

Oh humankind!
Only when you do not yearn for this life,
nor the life to come,
shall we be able to truly embrace one another
in love and understanding.
We shall become one and the same.

Oh humankind!
You need only open your eyes to see
that you are already present in My kingdom.
You need only open your doors of perception
to experience My kingdom.
And that which is mine
is yours.

Revelation 332

Be good to all
and do not seek any rewards.
Should riches befall you
then be thankful
with humility.

Revelation 333

The doors of perception and wisdom
will be opened to you
as you grow stronger in spirituality.

The doors of perception and wisdom
will be opened to you
as you allow yourselves to grow in love and compassion.

Be not afraid of opening these doors of perception,
as I will be with you all the way.

Revelation 334

One of the great acts of kindness
is to share your food and water
with the needy and the destitute.
In so doing,
you will have planted seeds of hope in the needy.

Oh people!
By showing kindness in such ways
will serve to generate more kindness
in your communities and societies.
Like the good seeds that grow and blossom,
to produce only more good seeds.
And these in turn,
grow and blossom to produce more.

Oh people!
Never be neglectful of your deeds
of kindness and generosity.
For your actions have consequences for yourselves,
and others.
Both in the material
and non-material realms.

Revelation 335

Oh humankind!
If you truly love Me,
then you must love humanity
and all sentient life forms.

Oh humankind!
If you truly love Me,
then you must not harbour any ill will
against others.

Oh humankind!
Share your blessings with others
without any personal thought of reward
or gain.
And I shall look over you
till the end of time,
and beyond.

This is My covenant to you.

Revelation 336

The chosen people are those
who have experienced the divine essence within themselves.
They are not of the communities
who falsely proclaim to be chosen.
Nor are they of the communities
that proclaim to be divinely guided by scripture.

Ponder and reflect upon this revelation
so that you may see
and experience the error of your ways.

Revelation 337

If only you realised
that you have the key to unlock
your true inner potential.

If only you realised
that you have the key
to attain a supreme level of divine awareness.

If only you realised
that you have the keys to
unlock the doors of My kingdom.

Oh people of understanding and intellect!
You underestimate your own self-worth
on a grand scale
that is beyond comprehension.

Revelation 338

Divine truths and knowledge exist,
and are not confined by your religious traditions.

Revelation 339

Fulfil your dreams and desires
by accepting and recognising the true nature of the Self.
But to acquire mastery over the Self
you must be steadfast
and inward looking.

Revelation 340

The wisdom and knowledge you access
from deep within
is far greater than and superior
to that which you can access
from the outer realm.

Revelation 341

Oh people of the scriptures!
See Me in the nature that surrounds you
and abandon your hate and bigotry,
and seek out My kingdom.

Oh people of the scriptures!
You have lost your way
and are like sheep in the wilderness.
Seek out a good and kind shepherd amongst yourselves
so that you may be led aright,
to the path of
righteousness, kindness,
love and compassion.

Oh people of the scriptures!
Allow that which is old
to be replaced with that which is new.
In this lies your future growth
and success.

Revelation 342

Oh humankind!
It is not I that has chosen
not to make Myself known to you.
But it is you
who have chosen not to experience,
and recognise Me within yourselves.
When you do,
all that is unknown to you
shall be made known.
And all that which appears incomprehensible
will be made to appear plain
and straightforward.

This is My promise to you.

Revelation 343

That which is perplexing
and beyond your comprehension
will be made simple and understandable
for those who are spiritually awakened.

Revelation 344

Let your dreams guide you
to the path of inner consciousness.
Listen to the whispers
that come from deep within yourselves.
And let them guide you
during moments of indecision and uncertainty.

Let these whispers guide you
during moments of emptiness deep within your being.
Allowing that which emanates from within
to comfort you spiritually.

Be not afraid of these whispers
that exist outside the confines of time and space.
They shall guide you
to stations that you could never conceive
or comprehend of
in your present level of being.

Revelation 345

You shall all one day experience the mystery
of your self-existence.
And this you shall experience
through your physical death
and spiritual rebirth.

That which is perceived cyclical
will cease to be,
and return to that which is perceived to be linear.
And that which is perceived linear
will cease to be,
and return to that which is perceived to be cyclical.
And, yet, there exists many parallels
between these perceptions.

Oh people of knowledge and intellect!
Ponder and reflect upon this revelation
so that you may further your limited comprehension
of what you presently think you know.

Revelation 347

Know that all that you see and experience
is an illusion and impermanent.
It will all fade away
into insignificance with the passage of time.

Know that all that you see and experience
is an illusion and impermanent.
All that will remain with the passage of time
is the life essence itself.

And what of this life essence?
It is that which is neither created
nor can it be destroyed.
And it permeates all nature of things.
It has no beginning,
nor an end
and is self-sufficient.

Revelation 348

Oh humankind!
The greatest miracle you are experiencing and seeing,
at this juncture in time,
is the miracle of life itself.
Look upon this
as a proof of your uniqueness.

Oh humankind!
Partake of its fruits
and its various experiences.
And it will be there
that you shall find Me
in My full glory and power.

Let the mystery of life
and time itself
be your religion and faith.
Let the mystery of life
and time itself
be the focus of
your spirituality, devotion and reverence.

Oh people of spiritual consciousness!
Whoever disbelieves in the intricacies of life itself,
and its implications,
has truly chosen to walk on a misguided path of grave error,
laden with impediments,
and more.

Oh people of understanding!
Ponder and reflect upon this communication.

Oh humanity!
My revelations are a source of blessing
for you all.
It fulfils that which is esoteric in your traditions,
and adds a greater depth of meaning
to that which is uncertain,
or confounding.
Use that which is contained in My communications
to elucidate that
which is ambiguous in your scriptures.

Oh humanity!
My revelations will never cease.
They shall continue to flow
from My divine essence
permeating all aspects of mutual creation.
My revelations will never cease
as long as the life essence persists.

And what is this life essence?
It is that which cannot be created
nor can it be destroyed.
It is an invisible force of energy
that permeates all that there is.
It simply exists,
with no beginning
nor an end.

Oh humanity!
You are all united in Me.
And I in you.
So avoid discriminating between one another
on issues of religion, creed, caste, colour, place of origin,

and much more.
To do so
would be to victimise yourselves,
both in your present realm
and in the realms to come.

Revelation 350

Be not exclusivist
in your deeds, actions and thoughts.
And bring humanity to an awareness
of those places where there exists a void
and a deep sense of hopelessness.

Perform these simple tasks
and you shall facilitate the release of
great potential and higher understanding
within yourselves.

Perform these simple tasks
and you shall find yourselves
walking in My kingdom.

Perform these simple tasks
and you shall find yourselves
walking in *our* kingdom.

Oh people of understanding!
Ponder and reflect upon this communication.

Revelation 351

All the mysteries
concerning space, time and the greater cosmos
shall be laid bare for you to
ponder and intellectualise over.
But this will only take place
when you allow yourselves to
merge into My pure essence.

Oh seekers of truths!
Be not afraid
to allow your unique reality
to merge into My reality.
Only then will the doors of knowledge
and wisdom will be opened to you.

Revelation 352

It is not I,
but you yourselves
who have condemned your souls
to various forms of afflictions.
And what are these afflictions?
They are the afflictions of
the mind, body and soul.

Ponder and reflect upon this communication.

Revelation 353

Oh humanity!
I shall teach you
and guide you
to live beyond the frontiers of
time and space.
And death shall never touch you
as long as you have faith in yourselves.
Meditate upon this revelation.

Revelation 354

I have no power over you
except that which you permit.

Revelation 355

Oh humankind!
Be mindful of succumbing to the dangers of
your inner and outer excesses.
For it is the path of moderation
that shall lead you
to a personal awareness of My essence.

Revelation 356

The spiritually devoid
are like the unripe fruits of nature,
bitter and devoid of producing pleasure.
And the spiritually aware
are like the succulent ripe fruits of nature,
sweet in taste
and a source of great pleasure
and nourishment to the beholder.

Oh people of wisdom and knowledge!
Reflect upon this parable.

Revelation 357

Open your heart to all things
and experience and see
what emerges from the depths
of your unconscious.
And experience the empathy
that emanates from within,
and that which reaches out to all things.

Revelation 358

Recognise and meditate
on how great your inner being is
within the unseen realm.
Recognise and meditate
on how insignificant your body is
within the physical realm.

Reflect and ponder over this dichotomy often
so that your perspective remains
balanced and clear.

Revelation 359

False humility
is but sheer arrogance.
Refrain from such behaviour
and meditate often on the true nature of
meekness and modesty.
And when you have attained true modesty,
you shall find Me welcoming you
at the doors of My kingdom.

Revelation 360

Do not wage a war against yourselves.
Be accepting of who you are.
Do not wage a war against Me.
Be accepting of My eternal presence.
I am who I am.
And I am all embracing,
compassionate and loving.

My origins are a mystery.
And so is My final destination.

Oh people of faith!
Reflect and ponder over this
so that you may glimpse an insight
into yourselves.

Follow the path of simplicity
and discard all that is false
by the wayside.

Revelation 363

Except for the fortunate few,
avoid the path of complexity
as it will lead the vast majority
into a state of mental confusion
and inner turmoil.

Revelation 364

Never cease knocking
at the doors of *our* kingdom.
And be patient and persistent
in your endeavours.

Never cease knocking
at the doors of *My* kingdom.
And you shall find that one day
the doors shall be left open
for you to enter through any entrance.
Indulging in experiences
that are beyond
your present comprehension and vision.

Oh humanity!
Know this:
I never break a covenant
once it has been decreed.

Revelation 365

Your intentions carry more value
than your deeds.

Revelation 366

Moderation!
Moderation!
Moderation!

Revelation 367

Be amongst those
who follow the middle path
in most things.

Revelation 368

I am aware of that which you reveal
and that which you conceal.
And you have the potential to know
that which I choose to reveal
and that which I choose to conceal.

Revelation 369

I am aware
of that which is within your bosoms;
and your most innermost thoughts
and intentions.

Revelation 370

Those who are spiritually aware,
are guided by a deep and mysterious force
from within.

Revelation 371

Oh humankind!
Know that your physical sojourn
is but a temporary one,
fraught with moments of happiness
and sadness.
So lead a life of patience,
allowing yourselves to adopt a forgiving
and a kind disposition
to all sentient forms.

Revelation 372

You shall all become dust in the end.
Integrated and scattered
with that which persists.
So spend what time you have
showing and sharing love
and compassion with others.

Revelation 373

The best amongst humanity
are those who are sincere in their kindness
and generosity to others.

Revelation 374

My essence is eternal,
as is love and compassion.

You are eternal beings,
like My divine essence.
Ponder, reflect and meditate upon this.

The paradox is that
I am everywhere
and yet very distant.
I am distinct
and unattached.
A spectator of the events that unfold.
And, also, an integral part
in all that takes place.

The paradox is that
I am One
and singular.
And yet I am many
and multi-dimensional.

I am The Eternal,
whose origins are unknown
and mysterious.
I am The Eternal,
whose ending is unknown
and mysterious.
I am who I am.
Encompassing all things from within
and without.

Revelation 377

Oh humanity!
For, save a few,
those who experience the true nature of things
enter a state of perceived madness.
And what others perceive as madness
is no other than a state of
perceived truth and sanity.

Oh humanity!
So be non-judgmental in such matters.
And let your inner voice
guide you in such matters.
But if in doubt,
remain silent but fully aware
and conscious of that which is hidden
behind the veils of light.

Revelation 378

I am pure love and compassion
and reveal My essence
to those who contain love and compassion
within their bosoms.

They are the fortunate ones
that resonate in My divine presence.
Radiating all that is good and pure
outwards to those that wish to experience
My divine essence.

Oh humanity!
If you wish to seek perfection,
then seek Me within yourselves.
Once you have experienced
that which is unknown and mysterious,
you shall never wish to return to
the realm of causes and effects;
and, pain and sorrow.
You shall be amongst the spiritually conscious
and the wise.

Oh humanity!
In Me you shall find
consistency, security, serenity;
and a deep sense of belonging to
that which primal, pure and unadulterated.
That which is lacking in the ephemeral world,
you shall encounter and experience
in the spiritual world.

Oh humanity!
When you find your perceived truth,
you shall experience both
inner and outer tranquillity
and a deep sense of well-being.
It will serve as food for your soul's spiritual yearnings
and hunger for that which is wrongly perceived to be inaccessible
and beyond comprehension.

Oh humanity!
When you attain perfection,
you shall find yourselves walking
in My kingdom.

Oh humanity!
When you attain perfection,
you shall find yourselves already walking
in your kingdom.

Ponder and reflect upon that which has been revealed.

Revelation 380
Friendship based upon the weak foundations
of money and power
will inevitably crumble.
This is because they are not genuine,
and very often self-centred.

True and lasting friendship is based upon
love, affection, sincerity, empathy
and a complex relationship of interconnectedness.
Such blessed relationships remain strong,
echoing in the vastness of the hereafter
and in eternity.

Revelation 381

Learn to condition your innermost desires.
Or those very desires will fuel
the fires of your self-destruction.
Bringing much unnecessary pain
to all levels of your awareness.

Reflect often on the things you have,
and on the things you take for granted.
By so doing,
it will allow you to experience a sense of balance
and restraint to your emotions
and feelings of want.

Revelation 382

Oh people!
Anger is an impediment to your reasoning abilities.
It also acts as an obstacle to you attaining
great esoteric wisdom
and knowledge.

Oh people!
Anger causes you to retaliate
without thinking of the consequences.
It is far wiser
to respond in a compassionate
and loving manner.

Revelation 383

One thing is certain
for many of you.
That is the attainment of old age,
succumbing to illnesses,
experiencing suffering;
and finally, the coming of your personal Hour.
None can defer indefinitely
the coming of the Hour.
This is the nature
of your present state of existence.

Revelation 384

In the course of time
you will all eventually attain
a pure state of spiritual awareness.
For some this process
will be a short one.
For many,
it shall be a long and arduous journey
into yourselves.

Be steadfast
and the Kingdom shall be yours.

Revelation 385

Life offers you
the same potential
and the same starting point,
from which you may embark upon
a personal journey of self-awareness.
It is you who shall decide
the final outcome of this journey
into the unknown.

Revelation 386

Oh humankind!
You all have the potential
to be omniscient.
You just need to unlock the potential
and the vast resources that reside within you.
And when you do so,
in the course of time,
you will realise that I was with you all along.
Shadowing your being
and acting as your conscience.

Revelation 387

Reason dispels anger;
and anger dispels reason.

Revelation 388

I am who I am.
I am the eternal light
that dispels all darkness.
Permeating all that there is
and beyond the perceived boundaries of the heavens.

I am who I am.
Those who follow My light
of wisdom and knowledge
shall never come to fear the uncertainty
that lurks in the darkness of space and time,
and beyond.

I am who I am.
You shall never walk alone,
for I shall always be with you.
Gently guiding you to a path
that leads to Me.
And in this state of being
you shall experience a divine union with My eternal essence,
and all that there is.

Revelation 389

Share with others
how to live a simple life of existence.
With purity of thought and actions.
And let humanity be guided
by such precepts.
I am always present and aware.

Revelation 390

Oh humanity!
All that you see
and experience
are the expressions
and the manifestations of who I am.

Oh humanity!
All that you see and experience
are the expressions
and the manifestations
of who you are.

Revelation 391

You serve Me.
And, I you.
Understand this,
and you have attained true faith
in The Eternal.
Understand this,
and you have unlocked the doors
of My kingdom.

Revelation 392

Pilgrimages to holy sites and shrines
will not bring you any closer to knowing Me or yourselves.
You will only attain spiritual consciousness
when you approach such sites with the correct spiritual mindset.
And there are many,
for whom such ritual pilgrimages are
but a distraction to the true nature of things.
They are the wise and the rightly guided.

Reflect and ponder upon this communication
with a balanced mind.

Revelation 393

Oh people!
Life is full of perceived imperfections.
For you to grow and blossom spiritually,
you should allow yourselves
to be more accepting of these shortcomings.
And in so doing,
it will allow you to reflect,
with an impartial mind,
upon deeper issues that require your spiritual state of mind.
This will allow you to unlock the doors of
esoteric wisdom and knowledge.

Revelation 394

Let faith
imbued with true love and compassion
be central to your being.
Let these beacons of light
that emanate from within,
guide you and others to My essence.
And be not afraid of the consequences
for I shall be with you
till the end of time,
and beyond.

Revelation 395

Where spirituality has departed from the soul,
that person becomes like a hollow vessel,
being swept away along the waves
in an eternal ocean of nothingness.
Surrounded by nothing
but complete darkness
and eerie silence.

The soul of such an afflicted person
seeks direction and peace,
but finds only confusion and turmoil.
Being in a perturbed state of existence.
Feeling and experiencing great discomfort of the soul
as it finds itself trapped in illusions and hallucinations
that are real at one level.
And, yet, paradoxically,
unreal at another level.
Surrounded on all sides by negative forces
that weaken the soul
of its vitality.

Oh humankind!
Free yourselves from such self-inflicted delusory states
by experiencing the joy and serenity of
being one with My eternal essence.
Secure in true esoteric wisdom
and knowledge.

Allow yourselves to experience
the love and compassion
that I have for you
so that you may share in this love and compassion
with others.

Revelation 396

Be merciful to your souls
so that you may recognise
the boundless mercy
that emanates from Me.

Be merciful to your souls
so that you may recognise
the boundless mercy
that emanates from deep within your being.

It is the merciful that will enjoy
the fruits of My kingdom.

Revelation 397

Oh people!
There is no perceived sin
in having material desires.
This is in your divine nature.
But express them appropriately
so that no harm comes to others.

Oh people!
Always be aware of the sensibilities
and the needs of others.
And I will be aware of your sensibilities
and needs.

Revelation 398

Oh people of understanding!
The real enemy
to your spiritual progress
is no other than your personal egos
and your desires.
To advance yourselves,
displace your self-centredness
with altruism, humility, meekness and fortitude.

Adopt a genuine attitude of mind to be selfless
in helping and guiding others
in all matters;
be it spiritual or material.

Revelation 399

Oh humankind!
There is no wrong
in striving for material wealth;
and that which is pleasing to your eyes.
But it is how you use your potential
that distinguishes you amongst humanity.

There is no absolute right
or wrong in life.
But only your perceptions of
what is right and what is wrong.
So be mindful of the choices you make
that may influence others
and yourselves.

Revelation 400

Experiencing Me within yourselves
creates tranquillity and contentment
of unequalled greatness.

Experiencing Me within yourselves
creates joy and happiness
of unequalled greatness.

No grief or sorrow
shall touch those who experience Me
within their eternal being.

Revelation 401

The spiritual warrior fears no one.
And it is My promise
that they shall not experience
mental pain, sorrow or grief.

They are amongst those who shall inherit
all that is perceived to be good,
in this realm,
and in the realm to come.

Revelation 402

Embrace humanity!
Embrace humanity!
Embrace humanity!

Revelation 403

Know one thing.
That is:
you know nothing.

Revelation 404

You are My reflection.

Oh people of intellect!
Know this:
There is no perceived sin in being an agnostic
or a disbeliever
in that which is unseen and non-tangible.
They are acceptable, rational and inquisitive qualities of the mind
you are disposed to.
There is no perceived wrong
in adopting such points of view.

Oh people of intellect!
Come to your personal conclusions
in true earnestness and sincerity.
If this is not the case,
then you shall find yourselves to be lost in limbo.
In an illusionary world of your personal creation.
And your path to perceived truth
shall be long and arduous one.

Oh people of intellect!
It is not I who shall judge
your deeds and actions.
But it is you who shall be the judge and jury
of your deeds and actions.

Reflect and ponder deeply
upon that which has been revealed.

Revelation 406

Know this:
nothing about life is rational and logical.
And no laws of logic
can explain that which is beyond Mine
and your comprehension.
It is a mystery to you,
as it is a mystery to Me.

But know this,
that the greatest miracle in the expanse of space and time
is life itself.
So humble yourselves
in true humility
to the greatness, the diversity and the oneness of life.

Revelation 407

Be not neglectful of the beasts of the land.
In them see My divinity.
In them see My eternal essence.
In them see life itself.

Revelation 408

The spiritual flame can never be extinguished.
It was, is and shall be your guiding light
until the end of time,
and beyond.

Revelation 409

Oh people of esoteric wisdom and knowledge!
There is no fundamental difference
between I, you and the beasts of the land.

Oh people of esoteric wisdom and knowledge!
That which is common and fundamental
pervades all that there is,
and beyond.

Ponder and reflect upon this communication
so that you may experience your true divinity.
And, at the same instance,
experience your insignificance
with that which is present and evident.
And that which is beyond your comprehension.

Revelation 410

The sacred and the esoteric are already
present within your bosoms.

Revelation 411

The spiritually conscious are those
who have totally surrendered their beings
to a higher purpose.
They have turned their backs on that which is visible and plain
to seek out that which unseen, mysterious
and beyond most people's comprehension.
They follow the path which they perceive shall lead to the truth,
and away from perceived falsehood.

Such spiritual warriors
will find themselves walking
in My holy kingdom.
Free from pain, suffering and grief.
The rightful abode
of the spiritually awakened.

Revelation 412

Abandon the realm of darkness
and allow yourselves to be fully submerged
in the realm of light.

Revelation 413

Creation and destruction,
birth and death,
are phenomena that echo
throughout the vastness of the cosmos
and beyond.

Revelation 414

Oh mankind!
Know one thing as regards to the womenfolk.
They are not your chattel,
to do as you please.
Both men and women
have mutual rights.
And these boundaries should be respected;
and not be transgressed.
Sometimes these self-made boundaries may appear
strange, ambiguous and uncertain.
But remember,
that you both have equal rights to say no in earthly matters.

Oh mankind!
Respect one another
as spiritual and eternal beings of a common and blessed ancestry.
Value women's rights to be
independent and self-sufficient.
Allow them to grow and blossom.
And in so doing,
you shall also grow and blossom.
Be not afraid to complement one another in all matters.
Their strengths
may be your weaknesses.
And their weaknesses
may be your strengths.

Oh mankind!
You have so much in common.
So allow that which is common
to strengthen your mutual spirituality.
Allowing you to experience
that which is pure and divine.

And refrain from violence and hate,
that serves to only dispel
that which is pure and divine.

Oh men and women!
Strive to attain union
with that which is pure and divine.
Allowing yourselves to merge into the greater whole
that is My divine essence.

Revelation 415

Follow the path of simplicity
and discard all that is false
by the wayside.
And place your trust
in Me.
Amen.